Play
as a
Learning Medium

Doris Sponseller, Editor

National Association for the Education
of Young Children
Washington, D.C. 20009

Photos:

Page viii: James Lattimer

Page 6: Bruce Grossman

Page 28: Dorothy Kay

Page 32: Betsy MacMillan

Page 52: Donna Harris

Page 58: a—Joy Crandall; b—Barbara Howe

Page 74: Marian Greenwood

Pages 80-107: Joel Fink, Oakland University Toddler Program and Child Care Center

Page 108: Elaine Wickens

Page 114: Jean-Claude LeJeune

National Association for the Education of Young Children
1834 Connecticut Avenue, N.W., Washington, D.C. 20009

ISBN Catalog Number 0-912674-42-3

Library of Congress Catalog Card Number 74-25866

Printed in the United States of America.

5/13/80 Berhear + Teyler 2.75

Dedicated to Matthew Lowry
whose untimely death was a loss
to all who value early childhood education.

Masculine and feminine pronoun references in this book are used only for editorial simplicity, and in no way reflect stereotyped concepts of children or adults.

Contents

The articles in this book are based on original presentations delivered at the following times and places:

The Problem of Play: Educational or Recreational?
Bernard Spodek

Keynote address presented at the Oakland University Ninth Annual Preschool/Early Childhood Education Conference for Parents and Teachers, "The Dynamics of Play," on October 27, 1973.

Piaget, Play and Problem Solving
Irene Athey

Paper presented as part of a series of lectures entitled "Views on Play," September 14, 1973, Oakland University, Rochester, Michigan.

Dramatic Play as a Curricular Tool
Nancy E. Curry

Paper presented as part of a series of lectures entitled "Views on Play," December 3, 1973, Oakland University, Rochester, Michigan.

Designing a Play Environment for Toddlers
Doris Sponseller
Matthew Lowry

Paper presented at the Second Annual Symposium on Play, April 12, 1974, Georgia State University, Atlanta, Georgia.

Introduction: Why Is Play a Learning Medium?

The contributors to this publication have looked at the phenomenon of play from a particular perspective. They have viewed play as an essential medium for learning. This perspective is an affirmation of the positive contribution which play offers to all stages of life and all areas of development. Although our focus is primarily on the cognitive developmental role of play, it is recognized that play contributes to all types of learning, including social, cognitive, physical, and emotional learning. Learning through play occurs in every domain of the young child's life, precipitating changes in the child which may not be immediately observable but which are crucial foundations for later observable behavior.

In addition, this perspective is a response to the stress on early academic learning which has become a pervasive force in our society. When early learning is defined as being only academic learning, play is often taken out of the curriculum to achieve these goals. The elementary school years have traditionally valued "work" in the classroom and have relegated play to recess time only. Kindergarten teachers are reporting that with increasing emphasis on accountability for reaching early academic objectives, there is now less time for play in their classrooms. And often the movement toward "educational" content in the preschool is interpreted in ways which cause downgrading or even abandonment of play time in the preschool as well.

Parents are now told that their job is not to play with their child but to teach him. The free and easy play interaction between parent and child at play has been an important part of early learning about self, family, and society. In an effort to develop "teachable" activities for parents, play behaviors have sometimes been utilized for structured lessons. If this unstructured play is replaced by conscious efforts on parents' parts to be "teachers," much of the spontaneity and delight of parent/child play may be lost.

Since the importance of early experiences for optimum future development is recognized by the majority of educators, psychologists, and parents, there is a need to examine the importance of play in relation to learning. Thus, the questions to which this publication is addressed are these:

> If early learning and fullest intellectual development are major goals of our society, does play have any part in enabling these goals to be reached?

> If play is seen to be an important learning medium, how does the adult facilitate the types of play in young children which enable esential types of learning to occur?

The value of play does not lie in a specific set of methodological structured "play" practices to teach specific skills. Play is valuable to the young child primarily as a medium for learning. The word **medium** can be defined in a number of ways, and a discussion of five definitions given by Webster (1969) can help us see why play can be viewed as a medium.

1. A medium is "a condition in which something may function or flourish."

    Play can be thought of as a condition in which learning may flourish and the cognitive structures of the mind can be allowed to function optimally, thus promoting the interaction of structure and function from which adaptive intelligence is created.

2. A medium is "a means of effecting or conveying something."

    Play is often the means by which the child's thoughts and feelings are conveyed, facilitating understanding of thoughts and feelings by the child. Since the young child is less able to use "internal" language as a means of conveying and understanding the complexity of his thoughts and feelings, the play medium provides a means of effecting his learning to himself.

3. A medium is "a channel of communication."

    Similarly, since the language which provides adults with their prime channel of communication is less available to the child, play often provides the channel by which thoughts and feelings are communicated to others. Many of the misconceptions of the child's understanding are made clear to adults through observations of play activities and the complexities of the child's learning are communicated through the channel of play.

4. A medium is "a surrounding or enveloping substance."

   Observers of young children are often aware of how completely enveloped the child becomes in play. Almost every activity in which the young child engages has elements of play behavior. Thus, play is a surrounding environment through which the child's learning is filtered.

5. A medium is "a material or technical means of active expression."

   In the young child active expression is vitally important; indeed, sensorimotor activity is a major mode of behavior. Play seems to be used by children as a technical means of actively expressing learning. Exploring a material from many perspectives, finding out all of the things which can be done with an object, playing out different ways to deal with a social situation all provide means of active expression of learning.

Thus, play can be defined as a medium through which learning occurs. But, for what types of learning is play the best medium, and how does it provide the optimum conditions for these types of learning?

The authors in this publication discuss the medium of play in relation to the specific kinds of learning with which each is primarily concerned. They also address the adult's role in facilitating the development of play as an increasingly rich medium for learning.

Bernard Spodek presents an overview of play's role as seen in the past and discusses the present theory and research concerning play as an intellectual and educative experience. He also discusses guidelines adults can use to be effective managers of the play environment.

Irene Athey examines the role play has in relation to the Piagetian view of the development of thought, not only as an abstract concept but as a viable, vital force in the problem-solving behavior of children. She suggests ways to enhance problem-solving skill development through play.

Nancy Curry deals primarily with the sociodramatic and social role learning aspects of play and their importance in symbolic learning. She indicates methods for encouraging sociodramatic play as a curricular tool.

Matthew Lowry and Doris Sponseller report on their observations of toddler play in a group setting and discuss how the center environment can be designed to facilitate growth in play behavior.

In addition, Doris Sponseller presents a schema for categorizing play and learning. Observational examples of specific types of learning which may be facilitated by the medium of play are included in four sections. These observational examples were provided primarily by graduate students in Early Childhood Education at Oakland University. Student contributors were Doris Bayburt, Rose Debra Berlin, Pam Boyle, Andrea Burger, Judith Bush, Kay Day, Vivian Olive, Phyllis Johnson, Rick Kamm, Cathy Noffert, Susan Simons, Sheila Steers, Joanne Wood, Virginia Woodworth, Lucille Smith, Kathy Grober, Jane Glotzhober, Nora Drozan, and Michael Kowalski.

Doris Sponseller
Editor

Bernard Spodek
University of Illinois

The Problem of Play: Educational or Recreational?

One of the interesting characteristics of the field of early childhood education is the need to justify our use of play in programs for children, as well as the need to justify ourselves as professionals whose prime concern is children's play. How do you justify a serious concern with play in the puritanical world in which we live today? Often what we do is deny our concern with play by twisting the words around so that play is considered as something else. We say, for example, that "play is the work of the child," thus equating work with play and turning play into work. If we call play work, we can be serious about it, thus maintaining our professional self-esteem.

The problem with such obfuscation is that we miss the whole point by denying our real concerns. We should not hide the fact that we are concerned with play, that we are involved in helping children to play. We need to become serious about play **as** play. If play is legitimate, then it needs to be accepted within its own right without confusing issues. We need to see play in its proper form in order to use it wisely rather than hiding it.

The need to justify play has presented a problem to early childhood education for a long time. Very

7

often you will hear parents who will not send their children to nursery school saying things like, "Well, why bother to send a child to nursery school? All they do is play. It is silly to spend all that money, get up early in the morning and join a car pool just to have the children play." Similarly, if you are concerned with children who grow up in poverty, you will often hear professionals argue that the regular nursery school program does not work out for economically deprived children because of its heavy reliance on play. What low-socioeconomic level children really need, we are told, are direct instructional programs in the academic skills. Play programs, the argument continues, simply are not powerful enough to help these children learn. Play programs are essentially frivolous, we are told, and we need to get down to a real "hard-nosed pressure-cooker" program of education.

These points of view suggest essentially that play serves a recreational function. Seldom in our commonsense world do we view play as serving educational functions outside of early childhood education. Play is recreation, a form of relaxation, a way to take the pressure of the world of work off people —from a commonsense point of view. But play does serve an educational function. For the last century or more we have had play programs in early childhood education.

The first activity-oriented program in the history of early childhood education was begun more than 100 years ago when Frederick Froebel started programs of early childhood education in Germany. Froebel called his school for young children **kindergarten** to symbolize the care to be taken in helping children grow. Froebel devised his early childhood program based on observations of children. From these observations he abstracted the essential ingredients of childhood life and created a program from this. The set of materials he designed to support his program he called **gifts,** and the activities for children he called **occupations.** The gifts were objects, such as balls and cubes and rectangles and straws. The activities included paper-weaving, paper-folding and cutting, as well as arts and crafts activities such as we offer children in kindergarten today. But was the activity of the original kindergarten play? Even though Froebel uses the word freedom extensively in his writing, the prescription of activities were highly specific. Because the children had to do exactly what they were told, the activities cannot really be termed play.

In Italy more than a half century later, a young woman doctor named Maria Montessori also became involved in the problem of educating young children. Dr. Montessori's strategy for developing programs was much like Froebel's. She observed children in play and abstracted from her observations the essential ingredients of that play. She created the Montessori Method from these observations. Here was another activity-based program of education, but was it play? Even though children were involved in manipulating materials, the way in which the children were required to use the materials precluded play.

In both these early approaches to early childhood education, observation of play activities was used to determine program, but what the observer saw and the meanings gathered from the observations were interpreted through the theory brought to the observation and the purposes ascribed to the observations. In both instances programs were created which had activity without play.

Beginning with the development of the nursery school movement in England in the 1900s and the reform kindergarten movement in the United States at about the same time, there began acceptance of the legitimacy of play activity in early childhood education. With the reconstruction of the kindergarten and with the beginning of nursery schools, a breed of educators developed who did not observe children in order to abstract and reconstruct from their activities the essential ingredients of life and learning. Rather they observed children and saw that what children do in play is real, is vital, and has within it the potential for learning about the world. They saw that play is used by children for testing out ideas, for abstracting information, and for somehow operating on this information. The natural activities of children were valued by these educators and were supported and nurtured in early childhood programs. So began the inclusion of dramatic play activities in educational programs, the provision of a housekeeping area, the beginning of block building, the beginning of outdoor play activities for children, not as recreation but as a legitimate educational form. Contemporary early childhood education programs have, in most cases, added to what we know about play and children and have elaborated upon the possibilities of play-learning activities for children.

The play-education movement has continued and been expanded. But in spite of a tradition of over 100 years, we continue to ask the questions: Is play really legitimate as a school activity? Is play really an aid to learning or does play get in the way of learning? And especially in these last few years, we have been asking: Does play serve a function in the intellectual learnings of a child? I would like to focus on the following questions:

    1. What is play? (Can we define it?)

    2. Why do children play? (Not only can we

define it, but can we explain it?)

3. Can child's play serve educational purposes. (If we look at the consequences of play activities, what do we find?)

4. Can adults support educational play? (Can we have adult intervention without distorting play?)

Defining Play

Play is difficult to define. There are 59 definitions of play in <u>Webster's New World Dictionary</u> (1972). We use the word play in many ways in our everyday life. For instance, you might go to see a "play," which would be a dramatic performance. You could "play" a game. You "play" a musical instrument, which presents a sense of performance. When you "kid around," you "play." A pun is a "play" on words. I took our car into the service station to be repaired because the steering wheel had too much "play" in it. We even talk of "playing around." Attempting to define the word **play** in everyday use presents problems.

Educators and philosophers have attempted to define play, and they have come up with a range of definitions, thus compounding the problems. These are some of the examples Mitchell and Mason (1948) collected:

Froebel: The natural unfolding of the germinal leaves of childhood.

Hall: The motor habits and spirit of the past persisting in the present.

Groos: Instinctive practice, without serious intent, of activities which will later be essential to life.

Dewey: Activities not consciously performed for the sake of any result beyond themselves.

Curti: Highly motivated activity which, as free
          from conflicts, is usually, though not al-
          ways, pleasurable. (pp. 103-104)

There are many ways of defining play. Each definition has a different consequence in terms of how
we understand and interpret play.

Often we define play as something distinct from
work. We know that an activity is play, if it is not
work. But how do we know when an activity is
work? If we attempt to distinguish play from work
by looking at the nature of the activity in which an
individual engages, we will find that the same activity can be identified as work under one set of
conditions and play under another set of conditions. When my son plays football on Saturday
morning, it is play. When O. J. Simpson participates
in a football game on Sunday afternoon, there is little
that is playful about it. It is very serious business.
Similarly, if I hire someone to build a cabinet for me,
the cabinetmaker is working. If I decided to create
a cabinet in my basement workshop, the same activity would be seen as play. And there would not
be anything frivolous about it, by the way. It would
be very serious cabinetmaking. (Whether the consequences would be worthy or not is another con-
sideration.)

It is not the activity then, but the reasons for the
activity taking place which determine whether it is
play or work. The criteria for play are not observable. The criteria for "play" or "not play" are in-
ferred from the sources of satisfaction. Activity
done for its own sake is seen as play; activity done
for external reward, salary, or pay is work. But even
that criterion presents problems. If you look at people who really enjoy their jobs, there often is a
quality of playfulness that can be identified in their
work.

12

We can also use "seriousness" as a criterion for distinguishing work from play; work being a serious activity, and play being frivolous. Using this criterion, anything that is frivolous can be considered play. But if you look at children in their dramatic play activity, very often it is hard to find anything that is frivolous about it. Children's play is often as serious as anything that you can possibly observe.

The problem with these definitions and criteria is that they tend to be used in an "all or none" fashion. We tend to see activities as being either all work or all play, and to think that if something is work it cannot be play and if it is play it can not be work.

Eva Neumann, in The Elements of Play (1971), analyzed the literature on play and came up with some definitions and criteria of play. She concluded that you can judge an activity and determine whether it is play or not play by using three criteria, not as "all or none" criteria but rather in terms of where the activity is on a continuum from "work" to "play," with most activities falling somewhere in the middle. The three criteria are:

1. **Control.** There is a difference between internal control and external control of activities. To the extent that control is internal, it is play. To the extent that the control is external, it is work. In most cases the control is neither totally internal nor totally external. The only time a person can totally control his own play activity is when he is playing alone. As soon as more than one player is involved, there is a sharing of control and therefore a move from internal to external control for each individual.

2. **Reality.** Neumann also differentiates between internal reality versus external reality. One of the criteria of play is the ability of the player to suspend reality, to act "as if," to pretend, to make believe, to suppress the impact of external reality, to let the internal reality take over. To the extent that activity is tied to the real world, it stops being play. To the extent that one can act in an "as if" way, one is acting in a playful manner. There, too, however, most play maintains some tie with external reality.

3. **Motivation.** To the extent that an activity is internally motivated, it is play. As soon as the motivation is external it stops being play. Seldom is the motivation entirely internal or entirely external.

J. Nina Lieberman (1965) developed a set of criteria for what she considered to be "playfulness." According to Lieberman, all activities have a quality of playfulness to them. In her study she found playfulness related to divergent thinking, that is, the more creative thinker was also the more playful thinker. Lieberman's five criteria for playfulness were: **physical, social,** and **cognitive spontaneity; manifest joy;** and a **sense of humor.**

Why Do Children Play?

These present some useful criteria for play that would help us define it more clearly and communicate better about play. Unfortunately, clearer criteria and definitions do not help us to understand why **people** play and especially why **children** play, a

14

problem that psychologists have looked at for literally hundreds of years.

J. Barnard Gilmore, in "Play: A Special Behavior" (1966), identified the various theories of play, many of them dealing with the reasons why people play. He then categorized the theories into two classes: the classical and the dynamic theories of play. The classical theories, which are older, try to explain why people play. The dynamic ones accept the fact that people do play and attempt to explain the processes of play. Under the classical theories of play are the **surplus energy theory,** the **relaxation theory,** the **pre-exercise theory,** and the **recapitulation theory.** While many of these theories have been around for awhile, we continue to use them in our common-sense discourse about play, even within the profession.

The **surplus energy** theory postulates that there is a quantity of energy available to the organism and a tendency for the organism to expend that energy either in goal-directed activity, which becomes work, or a goalless activity, which becomes play. Play occurs at any time when the organism has more energy available than it needs to expend for work. Within this theory, then, content of play activity is not important and one form of play could easily be substituted for another. The energy that people have is expended somehow, and if it is not expended at work, it is expended at play.

There is a kind of commonsense support for the surplus energy theory. If you have an eight-year-old son at home and you watch him on a rainy day when school is out, you have a "gut level" sense that there must be some validity to the surplus energy theory of play. The energy seems to build up until the child is ready to explode and all manner of activity seems to burst forth. But, when you try to look at the theory as a scholar rather than as a parent, it is hard to support this theory, for it cannot account for all the many situations in which play occurs.

According to the **relaxation theory,** play is used to replenish expended energy. It is a recreational form that allows you to gather additional energy to be used for work. The relaxation theory is more difficult to ascribe to young children's play than is the surplus energy theory. Young children do not engage in work activities from which they must relax. In fact, there is no real work for children in our society.

The **pre-exercise theory** suggests that play is instinctive behavior. The child instinctively involves himself in play activities which are in essence a form of some more mature behavior he will later have to assume. The content of the play is, therefore, determined by the content of mature, future adult activity. Play becomes a preparation for future work. For example, the play of little girls with dolls may be viewed as preparation for an adult mother role.

There is again some commonsense support for this theory. If you look at preliterate learning societies, for example, you may find that the children do a lot of running and shooting of bows and arrows, which, in the old days, paralleled the activity of adult hunters. The play of the boys could be explained as preparation for the male adult world. However, in our present society few of the many adult-role activities have their parallel in the play of young children. Indeed, the fact that many present vocational roles were not even conceived of during our childhood would raise serious questions about the validity of this pre-exercise theory.

The **recapitulation theory** suggests that rather than anticipating activities that will be essential in later life, play allows the individual to recapitulate the activities of earlier stages in the cultural develop-

16

ment of the race. Play, by allowing individuals to rid themselves of primitive and unnecessary instinctual skills, prepares them for the elaborate sophisticated activities of the contemporary world. The play of children is closer to the activities of primitive people than to mature adults, according to this theory.

The four classical theories seem to be composed of contradictory pairs, each attempting to explain the reason for the existence of play in human activities. The **surplus energy theory** provides an explanation of play that is contradicted by the **relaxation theory,** for one activity cannot both provide a means for sloughing off excess energy and a means for creating new energy. Similarly, while the **pre-exercise theory** explains play in terms of preparation for the future, the **recapitualization theory** sees the roots of child's play in the past, again a set of contradictions. None of the classical theories of play provide an adequate base for explaining the causes of play in all situations, nor do they adequately explain the existence of any content or thematic materials in the play of children.

The more modern theories of play were characterized by Gilmore as dynamic theories. There are two dynamic theories of play; one derived from psychoanalytic psychology, the other from Piagetian theory. The psychoanalytic theory considers play a cathartic activity which allows children to express and master difficult situations. Children can use the fantasy play situation to act out adult roles, which provides a feeling of mastery in fantasy situations and makes it possible to cope with reality. They can play out personally painful occurrences and by mastering pain in fantasy come to grips with it in reality. The same mastery of fantasy can allow children to cope with the affective elements of more positive life situations

17

as well.

Lois Murphy, in The Widening World of Children (1962), presents vivid descriptions of how young people use play activities to cope with the problems of living, such as starting nursery school or going to the hospital. Other difficult childhood experiences such as having a new baby within the family, having a fight with a friend, or even going through a harrowing Halloween experience can be played out until the child masters it, copes with it, internalizes whatever has been learned and can move on to deal with other kinds of things.

The psychoanalytic theory of play has had major consequences for early childhood education. When I first trained professionally, the role of the nursery teacher was that of a stage setter who never interfered with the play activities of children. The play activities would serve as catharsis, thus allowing the child to avoid fixation and an adult neurotic state. The children needed to play out their problems, and the teacher as an observer would take copious notes in order to understand but not interfere with their behavior. In those days the role of the nursery school teacher was very close to that of a child therapist.

More recently the works of Jean Piaget have been used to understand play. Piaget viewed the development of human intellect as involving two related processes: assimilation and accommodation. In the process of assimilation the individual abstracts information from the outside world and fits that information into the organizing schemes representing what he already knows. The individual also modifies these organizing schemes when they do not fit adequately with his developing knowledge. This later process is called accommodation.

Play, according to Piaget, is a way of taking the

outside world and manipulating it so that it fits the person's present organizational scheme. As such, play serves a vital function in a child's developing intellect and continues to some extent in adult intellectual behavior. Theory development, for example, is a form of playing. One suspends reality and deals with hypothetical situations, assimilating and accommodating in the process.

Piaget has defined three distinct stages in development of play. The first is the sensorimotor stage of infancy, based upon existing patterns of physical behavior. The second is a level of symbolic play, the stage of dramatic play in which we find most nursery-kindergarten children. The third stage is the stage of playing games that have rules, representing the play behavior of older children. As children mature through the early childhood period, they engage in more of this role-playing behavior, developing more of a game orientation along with a lessening of the dramatic play.

Given a Piagetian view, play can be conceived as representation. Once a child represents the outside world, the elements within it can be manipulated using the processes of assimilation and accommodation. Play then becomes an intellectual activity.

Michael Ellis, in his book, Why People Play (1973), adds another dimension to the theory of play. He characterizes as modern theories of play, those theories which view play as a function of competence motivation, and those that view play as an arousal seeking device. Traditionally, psychological theories conceive of the natural state of man as passive. Theories therefore need to be developed to explain activity. White's (1973) theory of competence motivation suggests that people receive satisfactions from developing competencies, independent of whether external rewards are gained in the process or not. Play is one way that children act on their environment, becoming more effective in their actions and thus receiving personal satisfactions.

Arousal seeking theory suggests that the human being normally needs to be continually involved in information processing activities. The absence of stimuli in a person's environment will lead to discomfort, therefore leading the individual to increase the amount of perceptual information available, either by seeking it externally or by creating it internally. Too much stimulation will lead an individual to "turn off" his environment by attending to it less. Play is a vehicle with which a child can mediate the amount of stimulation available to him in order to achieve a balance at some optimal level.

With arousal seeking theory providing an understanding of the child's move in creating exciting environment through play, and a Piagetian theory providing a system to explain the ways in which the child acts upon these stimuli through play to achieve knowledge, we can find theoretical justification for the uses of play as an educational tool.

Play Can Serve Educational Functions

We want young people to become something different than they would become naturally, so we put children in an artificial, contrived situation that we call "the school," and we intervene in their development. This intervention is called education. Teachers intervene this way, as do mothers, nondirective therapists, and even those people who believe in the free school movement. Sometimes our interventions are explicit, sometimes they are implicit, sometimes direct, and sometimes indirect. But no matter how we intervene, we ought to be doing so consciously. If intervention is done consciously, it can be done carefully, it can be done well, and it can be done easily.

20

The question is, can we have intervention (education) and play at the same time? Let us go back to the three criteria suggested by Neumann (1971): internal versus external control, internal versus external reality, and internal versus external motivation. The extent to which the child still has a degree of control over the play situation determines its degree of reality and provides motivation for the activity. To that extent the activity is play. As long as the child can decide whether to be involved or not, when to start and when to stop his involvement, and when to switch activities, it continues to remain play. But in educational play, the teacher also has a degree of control, also influences the child's motivation, also imposes a degree of reality on the play of children. When does the activity stop being play? When have we gone too far with our interventions?

Ellis (1973), using the Neumann criteria, suggests a number of pairs of questions that you can ask about it:

1a. Is the child undertaking the behavior in order to achieve a payoff? or
1b. Is the child behaving only for the experiential rewards associated with the process?

2a. Is the behavior controlled by somebody other than the child? or
2b. Is the child controlling the behavior?

3a. Is the child forced by circumstance to recognize all the constraints of reality? or
3b. Is it possible for the child to bend some aspects of the real situation by suspending temporarily associations between events in favor of an imagined situation?

4a. Does the setting or situation, including adults, impose consequences that by requiring given behaviors prevent children's concern for the process of their behavior?
4b. Does the setting provide interactions that are

freed from an externally applied final consequence?

5a. Is something in the setting so constraining the behavior that the choices among responses available to the individual are limited?

5b. Does the setting permit the choices at each choice point in a stream of behavior to rest with the individual?

6a. Does the setting prevent a relaxation from a concern with the real connections between events and consequences? or

6b. Does it allow the suspension of some aspects of reality?

All of these questions are general and are rather redundant but they bear on the extent to which the child can be characterized as working or playing in the sense that his behavior is externally or internally determined. At this point it must be re-emphasized that no setting can be so arranged that a child can be totally freed from external constraints. What is expected to result from the questions is the removal of unnecessary constraints so that there is an improved probability that the child will emit the kinds of responses that seem to be driven by the need to play. (pp. 125-126)

How Do We Support Educational Play?

Both teachers and parents consciously or intuitively guide play. Burton White et al., in Experience and Environment: Major Influences in the Development of the Young Child (1973), reports a study of children in their early years of life and the family influences that seemed to help them become more or less competent. In their conclusions, White and his associates present some of their best guesses about most effective childrearing practices:

Our A mothers talk a great deal to their children, and usually at a level the child can handle. They make them feel as though whatever they are doing is usually interesting. They provide access to many objects and diverse situations. They lead the child to believe that he can expect help and encouragement most, but *not all* the time. They demonstrate and explain things to the child, but mostly on the child's instigation rather than their own. They prohibit certain activities, and they do so consistently and firmly. They are secure enough to say "no" to the child from time to time without seeming to fear that the child will not love them. They are imaginative, so that they make interesting associations and suggestions to the child when opportunities present themselves. They very skillfully and naturally strengthen the child's intrinsic motivation to learn. They also give him a sense of task orientation, a notion that it is desirable to do things well and completely. They make the child feel secure.

Our most effective mothers do not devote the bulk of their day to rearing their young children. Most of them are far too busy to do so; several of them, in fact, have part-time jobs. What they seem to do, often without knowing exactly why, is to perform excellently the functions of designer and consultant. By that I mean they design a physical world, mainly in the home, that is beautifully suited to nurturing the burgeoning curiosity of the one- to three-year-old. It is full of small, manipulable, visually detailed objects, some of which were originally designed for young children (toys), others normally used for other purposes (plastic refrigerator containers, bottle caps, baby-food jars and covers, shoes, magazines, television and radio knobs, etc.). It contains things to climb, such as chairs, benches, sofas, and stairs. It has available materials to nurture more mature motor interests, such as tricycles, scooters, and structures with which to practice elementary gymnastics. It includes a rich variety of interesting things to look at, such as television, people, and the aforementioned types of physical objects. (pp. 242-243)

In essence, White suggests these parents provide a world for children to play in. Rather than teach directly at prescribed times, they do a lot of it "on the fly."

Teachers of young children, in many cases, use the same model for their role as these mothers did. They serve as designers and consultants in a dynamic classroom. They create a world in which children can learn through play, modifying play opportunities for children to increase their educational value.

Sylvia Krown (1974) describes such a model of teaching in her report on a program for disadvantaged children in Israel. Included in the report are delightful descriptions of how the play of the children changed during the program. In the beginning, play activities were highly stereotyped. Two years later, the children who have gone through this program have modified their play. The quality of richness within the play becomes evident in the descriptions.

What is it that these teachers did that effected change? There are at least four strategies reported in this study:

1.   The teacher spends time "startling children out of vagueness into purposeful activity." Sometimes the teacher might invite herself into the play by asking questions. "Is it a birthday?" "I want to be at the birthday, too; where should I sit?" "Where is the birthday cake?" She may then remove herself from the play.

2.   Sometimes, the teacher adds new materials to stimulate play. If the children, for example, were playing bus driver, the teacher might provide tickets to sell to passengers or a bell to ring when the passengers wish to get off. Simply taking a chalk line and marking a road on

the floor of the play area may be just enough to move the activities on to the next step.

3. Sometimes the teachers ask questions to stimulate more detailed observation and play, to help children recall and associate prior experiences.

4. Some teachers developed discussions to stimulate more detailed observations and play. Trips, books, and other ways of providing children with additional information to be used in their play were also provided by the teachers.

In these ways the children are still allowed to have control over their world, allowing them to maintain a sense of suspended reality, and allowing them to motivate their own activities with play. But the play was educational.

When does a teacher intervene? How far should you go in extending play? This is hard to judge except situationally. The judgment must be based upon a knowledge of children in general and the children in a particular play situation as well as a knowledge of the kinds of play activities that might be productive at a given time. Too much intervention will stop play or cause it not to be play. At the same time the absence of intervention can keep play from achieving its potential. The teacher has to continually work for some kind of balance in her relationship in the play situation.

Conclusion

The problem of play for teachers, parents, and recreational workers is to keep the activity "play" without distorting it, even while intervening, optimizing its educational consequences without losing the essence of play. Children can be seduced into games for adult purposes. They can mouth phrases far beyond their ability to comprehend. They can repress their needs, their desires, even their intellectual ability to please adults. All activities in a child's school and in his home need not be play and should not be play, and all activities in the home and school need not be educational. Teachers can impose and can distort or they can back off. They can also refuse to intervene and miss opportunities for learning. Without some help, children's activities can become repetitive, stereotyped, and devoid of educational consequences.

The key then is balance. Sensitive, provocative balance, design, and consultation can help move children's activities along so that their thinking moves along as well. Learning can occur in a context of playfulness. The essence of good teaching and good parenting for young children lies in this ability to think about the needs of young children, to respond, to intervene without unnecessary interference and distortion. Perhaps this requires adults who themselves bring a quality of playfulness as well as respect to their relations with children.

In sum, the problems of play may be as much the adults' problems as they are the children's. As we learn to understand the reasons for children's play and its consequences, perhaps we will see play as a potential, rather than as a problem.

References

Ellis, M. J. *Why People Play*. Englewood Cliffs, N.J.: Prentice-Hall, 1973.

Gilmore, J. B. "Play: A Special Behavior." In *Current Research in Motivation*, edited by R. N. Haber, pp. 343-

355. New York: Holt, Rinehart & Winston, 1966.

Krown, S. *Threes and Fours Go to School.* Englewood Cliffs, N.J.: Prentice-Hall, 1974.

Lieberman, J. N. "Playfulness and Divergent Thinking: An Investigation of Their Relationship at the Kindergarten Level." *Journal of Genetic Psychology* 107, no. 2 (December 1965): 219-224.

Mitchell, E. D., and Mason, B. *The Theory of Play* (revised edition). New York: A. S. Barnes & Co., 1948.

Murphy, L. *The Widening World of Childhood.* New York: Basic Books, 1962.

Neumann, E. A. "The Elements of Play." Unpublished Doctoral Dissertation, University of Illinois, 1971.

White, B. *Experience & Environment: Major Influences in the Development of the Young Child.* Englewood Cliffs, N.J.: Prentice-Hall, 1973.

Webster's New World Dictionary: Second College Edition. New York: World Publishing Co., 1972.

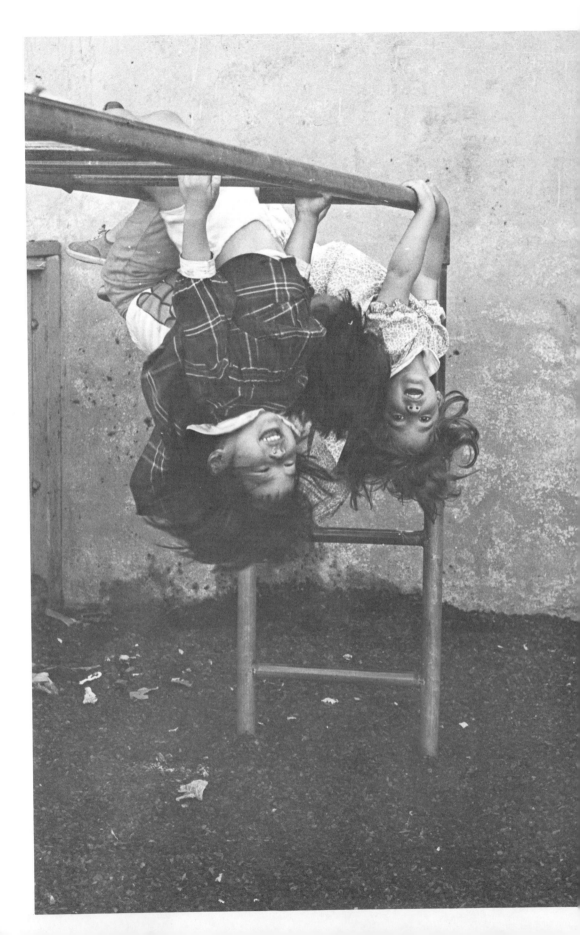

The role of play in learning physical and per-ceptual skills has long been recognized. Many of the young child's activities are practice play or simple self-imposed games. Children also play with language in their efforts to master both the symbols and the concepts to which these symbols relate. Often sensorimotor play and games utilize language play as well. Therefore, physical, perceptual motor, cognitive, and verbal skills may all be enhanced through the same play activity.

Skills-Enhancing

C., boy age four, in waiting room of doc-tor, fell on stomach, rolled over, and sat up. Used drawer pulls as door knockers. Laid down. Made noise like engine. Repeated while moving across floor in "lope"—arms together, legs together. Walked around aquarium dragging feet. Attracted another child, chased three times around. Mother stopped him. Walked, dragging feet. Moth-er stopped him. Watched fish. Looked through aquarium to another child, "You can't see me." Played peek-a-boo with a child at each end of aquarium, leaning from one side to another to peek. Crawled, drag-ging stiff legs. Child asked, "Are you crawl-ing like a dog?" Shook head and crawled on hands and knees.

Boy age four, girl age four, girl age three, working at the table with crayons and paper, R., four years old, had used scissors

29

to cut out a seahorse. J., four years old, had then made one similar to his. R. was coloring his seahorse and sing-songing. "I'm using the black crayon. I'm using the black crayon." J. joined in, "I'm using a black crayon, too." R. changed crayons. "Now I'm using the purple crayon too." L., three years old, had been a silent observer, but now said, "I'm using a purple too." "But that's not a crayon" observed R. "No," agreed L. "I'm using a purple magic marker." This sort of play went on for some time with one argument over whether one crayon was blue or purple, and ended with lining all the crayons up and chanting as the crayons were put in place. "This is blue one, this is red one, this is orange one," etc.

It is recess time; a group of boys, ages seven and eight, are near the slide. One goes up and slides down. Two other boys follow, they repeat, laughing. Now the first boy has a box. He gets it to the top of the slide. Positions the box. Steps in. Pushes off. Slides down laughing. Brakes himself at bottom. Runs back to ladder. Gets to top. Positions box; steps in. A second boy steps in behind him. Tries to sit. Box begins to tear. Pushes off. Box tears more. Reach bottom laughing. A group is gathering. Two boys tear the box apart and flatten it. They both try to carry box to top of slide. Some pulling. They get to top. One boy positions cardboard, tobogganlike. The two boys get on. A third squeezes on at back. Down they go laughing. More want to try. Back up they go. Five boys try to get on cardboard. Last boy only has his feet on it. Down they go.

One boy seems to be the leader; he is always at the front.

Two children, both two years old, had a large wagon with removable side boards. One child tried to get into the wagon but could not climb as high as the wagon. She then discovered she could remove the front and climb into the wagon. She climbed into the wagon, sat down, and then the boy got into the wagon with her. They sat there for a few moments, then the boy climbed out, picked up the wagon handle, and began pulling the girl down the walk. He turned around and returned with the wagon to the spot where they got into the wagon. The riding child got out and the boy climbed into the wagon and sat down. The girl pulled the wagon down the walk and returned as the boy had done. This continued for about 20 minutes.

When my six-year-old was younger, I used to read him Johnny Crow's Garden, quite often, but I hadn't done so in a long time, so I chose it recently. My three-year-old climbed up on the sofa to listen with us. R. remembered the story at once and insisted on reading all the pages which said, "In Johnny Crow's Garden." A few days later I noticed S. with the book. She was reading aloud as she so often does to nobody but herself. She turned the pages rapidly, talking about the lion and the hippopotamus and the monkey and the whale. Every two or three pages she would stop turning, slow down her speech, and state clearly, as her brother had, that it happened In Johnny Crow's Garden.

Irene Athey
University of Rochester, New York

Piaget, Play, and Problem Solving

Children spend a large portion of their waking time in play. There have been several theories about the functions of play in the growth and development of children.

Karl Groos (1916) theorizes that play is really practice for future adult functions. For example, the lion cub learns the techniques needed for hunting in the course of playing with other cubs. It is not immediately apparent how well this theory fits human children, because the adult functions they will later assume are so varied. Young children do imitate their elders a good deal in their play, of course, but it would be difficult to argue that when a little girl of four plays at tea parties she is actively practicing for a role as hostess 20 years in the future.

Piaget (1962) has pointed out another difficulty with the pre-exercise theory. This criticism concerns so-called "autotelic" activities (**telos, Gr.**—end, autotelic—an end in itself) such as the baby's sucking or smiling, which clearly mirror later adult activities. If pre-exercise were the criterion of play, we would have to say that practically everything the baby does constitutes a play activity. Hence, when a baby is lying quietly in a crib, looking intently at some object, and then refocusses his gaze on another object, we would have to say, according to Groos's theory, that the baby is playing at looking, in preparation for the times it will be necessary to concentrate his attention in adult life. Such a statement reduces the theory to absurdity.

Arguments like the above clarify the difficulty in defining exactly what we mean by play. Piaget (1962, pp. 89-90) talks about the exercise of activities for the mere pleasure of mastering them, without the expectation of results. We may need to qualify the last part of that definition, but let us keep it in mind, at least for the time being.

I believe, in agreement with Piaget, that play is the basis of all later cognitive functioning and is, therefore, indispensable in the life of the child and, to a lesser extent, the adult. Now this is a rather extreme and perhaps unpopular assertion at the present time. For example, some psychologists argue that play is an excellent medium for social learning (sharing toys, etc.), but that the school should be primarily, if not exclusively, concerned with cognitive growth, which they feel is induced through structured academic activities rather than play. Such a statement reflects a profound misunderstanding of the nature and function of play. Play is as vital to the development of cognitive functioning as it is to physical, social, or emotional growth.

To understand this, we should look more closely at Piaget's theory of representation. Adult intelligence, in all its manifest variations, is rooted in the symbolic function, i.e., the use of symbols to represent an object or another symbol. This ability is the essence of the operational processes which characterize scientific, mathematical, and logical thinking. Consider, by contrast, the sensorimotor intelligence of the very young child, which consists of actions and sensations. How does this type of intelligence evolve into the later type? Essentially it evolves through the development of meanings. Piaget (1962) notes, "there is functional continuity between the sensory-motor and the representational, a continuity which determines the construction of the successive structures." (pp. 2-3) Play, especially from the point of view of "meanings," can be considered as leading from activity to representation.

By looking at play and imitation, it is possible to trace the transition from sensorimotor assimilation and accommodation to the mental assimilation and accommodation which characterize the beginnings of representation. Here Piaget contrasts play and imitation, though both are important sources of representation. Assimilation is the process by which a person takes in reality and processes the intake in terms of his understandings at that time. People will assimilate what is essentially the same experience very differently at different ages. Accommodation refers to the changes which come about in one's behavior and thinking as a result of what has been assimilated.

You can see, I think, that either of these processes, if pushed to the extreme, might result in mental and behavioral aberrations. If assimilation was accomplished without accommodation, the person might evolve a perfectly logical system of thought which is almost entirely out of touch with reality. On the other hand, slavish accommodation to reality, without assimilation, would result in the possibility of becoming almost an automaton. I am not sure that either assimilation or accommodation can exist in pure form without the other. The nearest one can come is in imitation, which is almost pure accommodation, in which the imitator reproduces what exists in reality. In play, accommodation to reality is virtually suspended and assimilation is in the ascendancy. Needless to say, it is the balance or interaction, the equilibrium between the two, or rather the constant imbalance and redistribution at new levels of equilibrium that allows us to progress to new understandings while staying in tune with reality.

Another point to remember is that the young child's thinking is egocentric, so that meanings are extremely individualistic and subjective. While this is still true to some extent of adult thinking, by the time children reach the formal operational period at about age 11 or 12, their thinking has become socialized to the extent that there is a core of objectivity and common meaning which makes communication possible. Of course, this does not happen suddenly with the approach of adolescence. It is a long gradual process of emancipation from the completely subjective to the more objective.

An interesting feature of human development is that some characteristic may be based on, and grow out of, its opposite. For example, a child cannot learn to be independent without the previous opportunity to be dependent. Independence is based on security, or the feeling of dependence. Maturity does not consist in throwing off all dependencies and becoming completely independent, but rather in striking an appropriate balance. In somewhat the same way, thought progresses from the completely subjective to become increasingly objective while retaining some of the individualistic qualities which make for creativity, imagination, humor, and all the other facets which make a person unique.

Let us examine, then, the role of play in this long transition toward the end product of objective thought. Play, you recall, is almost pure assimilation, in which reality is subservient to the child's imagination. Play is the medium by which the child expresses not only needs, but also an understanding of experiences. Language is not suitable for such expression in this transitional period, because language presupposes the existence of the symbolic function, and the symbolic function is only beginning to emerge. At this stage, therefore, play is the primary vehicle for the expression of thought.

This point is worth emphasizing because many educators' misconceptions about the value of play may be based on the thinking of some psychoanalytic writers who have concentrated on the emotional value of play. Play has indeed proved to be a useful tool in the diagnosis and therapy of children's emotional problems, but it would be a mistake to conclude that the only contribution of play to cognitive learning is its indirect help in relieving the child of anxieties and guilt. Early childhood educators have recognized intuitively the intellectual value of play. The following outline will provide more precise documentation.

Sensory Learning

In an article entitled "Play is Valid" (1968), Lawrence Frank says of play and learning:

> With his sensory capacities, the child learns not only to look but to see, not only to hear but to listen, not only to touch but to feel and grasp what he handles. He tastes whatever he can get into his mouth. He begins to smell what he encounters. He can and will—if not handicapped, impaired, or blocked—master these many experiences through continual play . . . the most intensive and fruitful learning activity in his whole life cycle. (p. 435)

Such exploratory activity is the basis of rich concept formation, as well as the associations which permit children to form the cross-concept associations that are the foundations of generalizations and principles. Gagné has illustrated forcefully, in The

Conditions of Learning (1970), how dependent the understanding of principles is upon the concrete understanding of their component concepts.

It follows that from birth the child needs an environment rich in visual, auditory, and tactile experiences calibrated to his information-processing abilities at a particular stage. Bower's (1966 and 1971) research has shown that even infants a few weeks old can and do (1) discriminate visual patterns; (2) find complex visual patterns intrinsically more stimulating than color brightness alone; (3) recognize certain regularities in the environment, such as solid objects and faces; and (4) decrease their attention to familiar patterns and seek novel stimuli. In brief, the infant sees a patterned and organized world which can be explored actively with the limited perceptual abilities at his command. Industrial designers are now beginning to create enriched sensory environments for babies in recognition of this fact.

The preschool child needs an extension of the infant's enriched environment, but the stimulation will be of a different order. Here the children need materials which have their own intrinsic order and complexity, but they also need materials on which they can impose their own order and complexity—sand, water, clay, paint, and throwaway materials of every variety and in great abundance. Of course, it is possible to overstimulate a child by presenting a bewildering variety of too many and too distracting materials at any one time. The child needs a constant diet of paced novel stimuli, including novel ways to use familiar stimuli. Kagan (1968) has pointed out the importance of novelty as a challenge to cognitive growth.

Concept Formation

In addition to a rich sensory environment, preschool children also need materials tailored to their growing intellectual powers. Through exploration they learn about the properties of things under different conditions—how sand behaves when it is wet vs. dry, that glass can be made to bend when it is heated, that leaves and corks float, while marbles (which are smaller) sink. David Elkind, in "Piaget and Science Education" (1972), has suggested that teachers should capitalize on the preschool child's keen powers of observation and love of collecting to lay the foundation for the scientific attitude. At this age, the child is not only impelled by natural curiosity to explore and observe, but his powers of observation are not clouded by the assumptions and misconceptions that frequently characterize adult thought. A graduate student once told me that up into her high school days, she had always thought that hot water traveled more slowly than cold water, because the hot water always took longer to reach the faucet.

Such misconceptions are less likely to occur when the child has ample opportunity to observe the behavior of natural objects under a variety of conditions. This is what we mean by well-developed concepts. The definition or connotation of an object, e.g., metal, may consist of a few essential properties of the object. We are often willing to say that a person understands the concept if he can list the properties. But the denotation of the object consists of an infinite number of behaviors manifested by metals in relation to other objects or conditions. To provide children with the beginnings of this intricate network of interrelationships, beyond the mere identifying and labeling of objects, is to lay the foundations of future intellectual growth.

There are, however, concepts governing logical thought which are even more fundamental than the properties of objects, because they provide the formal structure of thought regardless of its content. These are the concepts with which Piaget has been particularly concerned. They include first the concept of transitive and intransitive **relationships.**

An example of a transitive relation would be $A=B$, $B=C$, $\therefore A=C$. An example of a transitive, asymmetrical relation would be $A>B$, $B>C$, $\therefore A>C$. Obviously this cannot be reversed, and still retain its truth value without changing the relationship to $<$. While this is obvious to adults on logical grounds, children must come to understand these relationships through concrete experience.

Allied with the notion of transitivity is the concept of order or **seriation,** based on a single property such as size, length, etc., or upon a combination of properties such as size **and** length. There is also the concept of **distance** both in space and time, and the concept of **speed** which relates both to space and time. A concept which has received much attention from research psychologists is that of **conservation** —conservation of number, of mass, of weight, and of volume. Piaget has described the intense excitement experienced by one of his mathematician friends when, as a child, he made the spontaneous discovery that the **number** of an array of objects (in this case pebbles) was independent of the order of the array. He found that he could lay the pebbles in a row and begin counting from either end, or he could place them in a circle and start from any point in the circle, with the same result. That learning episode, which came through his unstructured play, was so vivid that the memory of it stayed with him even as an adult.

There is the concept of **cause and effect** (obviously related to the idea of sequence of events) as it pertains both in the physical and the psychological

40

world. If it takes time to understand causal relationships in the physical world (remember our student and the hot water faucet), how much more difficult is it to infer the causes of complex human behavior.

When we do begin to understand these physical and psychological relationships, we have a basis for the concept of **probability,** the probability that one event will follow on a given set of other events. Since our lives and our fortunes are determined to no small extent by our estimations of the probability of certain events occurring—from the probability of finding a parking place in the morning to the probability of winning the state lottery—this concept is one of the cornerstones of logical thought.

Finally, we must include some of the component ideas which make up our concept of **morality,** including the notion of rules, of reward and punishment, of guilt and innocence, and of justice. All these concepts—relationships, seriation, space, time, speed and distance, conservation, causality, probability, and morality—constitute the structural basis of thought through which we process a great deal of the content of our intellectual lives. It is therefore essential that we provide the young child with sufficient number and variety of experiences that he can begin to induce these formal concepts for himself.

Hypothesis Testing

Those familiar with Piaget's work will recall that the final, formal-operational stage of learning differs from preceding stages in being characterized by hypothetical, deductive thinking. Again, we should be aware that this "if-then" type of thinking does not arrive full-blown when the child reaches a certain age, but has its roots in the way he has been encouraged to handle his earlier experiences. In <u>Intellectual Growth in Young Children</u>, Susan Isaacs

(1966) gives many examples of hypothetical reasoning by young children. She says:

> The abilty to evoke the *past* in imaginative play seems to me to be very closely connected with the growth of the power to evoke the future in constructive hypotheses. . . . (p. 104)

In other words, the ability to make fruitful hypotheses or correct predictions grows out of a correct understanding of past events. But it is through play that the child is able to assimilate or understand past and present events. Hence play is indispensable to the ability to formulate valid hypotheses.

Here are a few examples of hypothesis construction taken from Isaacs's book (pp. 112-113). The children, ranging in age from 2.8 to 8.6 were enrolled in an open school. (A description of the children and school appears on pp. 14-15.)

> Christopher put a thermometer into a jar of hot water, and Dan (5;0) told him (having used it the day before), "it goes up when you put it in hot, and goes down when you put it in cold."

> In the garden, the sun was hidden by a cloud for a few minutes. When it came out again, Phineas (4;0) remarked, "The sun's come out again. The sun makes it warm and cold, doesn't it? Now it's warm."

> Phineas (4;0) was blowing through a rubber tube in water, and watching the bubbles rise and break. Miss C. asked, "What's making the bubbles?" He said, "The wind in here" (pointing to the tube). "Where does the wind come from?" "From my mouth, because I'm blowing."

> While Dan (4;1) was sharpening a pencil, he talked to Mrs. I. about "marrying." He said, "I can't be married to a boy, and Priscilla can't be married to a lady." And then, "Priscilla can't be married to you, but I can. Yes, because you are a lady." But after a pause, "No, boys can't be married to ladies."

Sometimes lack of experience or misinterpretation of experience may lead to invalid hypotheses:

There is another facet to this matter, however. What do we mean when we say we want the child to become a problem solver? We hope he will be able to cope with all the kinds of problems he will meet in his life—personal, professional, and social problems—by using intellectual tools. But I think we mean more than this. We hope to create a generation of young people who will go out into the world and **find** problems to be solved, or even generate new problems and solutions. A good part of solving any problem lies in identifying and determining exactly what the problem consists of, what its dimensions are, and in hypothesizing the roots of the problem. This hunger for new problems, or new solutions to old problems, we might call "the problem-solving attitude." This attitude is, or should be, in my view, the primary aim of education.

Play can be an important means of inculcating this problem-solving attitude. There is a growing body of evidence which suggests that, in order to achieve in school or indeed in life beyond school, the individual needs to feel that he has some measure of control over his environment. There is a body of literature on the correlates of internal vs. external "locus of control," which you may remember as one of the variables cited in the Coleman report.

Early childhood educators familiar with Erikson's theory will recognize this control as Erikson's **mastery of the environment.** Erikson maintained that the lifelong feeling of mastery or control over one's physical and social milieu must be established at the primary school age, or probably not at all. Certainly this is a critical period, when the child is expected to acquire the tools of the society. But the seeds of this feeling are sown much earlier, probably from the earliest days of infancy.

The importance of play lies in the fact that play

represents a world in which the child can be master of whatever environment he chooses. No matter that physical objects stubbornly obey natural laws; in his imagination they can do whatever he desires.

In illustrating the progressive ritualization away from objects in make-believe play which makes the transition from object to symbol through progressive abstraction, Piaget (1962) remarks on "the feeling of efficacy" which accompanies such rituals. This feeling can be seen in the pleasure which children derive from repetitions of the ritualized action (p. 95).

> At about 1.3, J. learned to balance on a curved piece of wood which she rocked with her feet, in a standing position. But at 1.4 she adopted the habit of walking on the ground with her legs apart, pretending to lose her balance, as if she were on the board. She laughed heartily and said "Bimbam." At 1.6 she herself swayed bits of wood or leaves and kept saying Bimbam, and this term finally became a half generic, half symbolic schema referring to branches, hanging objects, and even grasses. (p. 96)

Notice how J., without adult intervention, is forming a class of swaying objects which includes anything hanging (beginning of formation of a principle) and also herself in certain positions. Notice the rapidity with which this generalization takes place, and the pleasure she derives from extending her learning to new objects.

Symbolic play is an excellent vehicle for learning. Through it the child expresses his understanding of the way things and people behave, but he may also come to revise some of his concepts in the light of his play experience. Spontaneous discussion arising in the course of play will serve to correct some misconceptions. This discussion is often a testing ground for digesting partially understood information obtained from adults. In fact, Piaget maintains that it is through repeated interactions of this kind with peers that the child's thought becomes progressively socialized.

Symbolic play serves another function in the child's cognitive life, which may be called "putting himself in the role of the other." Because he can switch roles at will, being now the driver, now the passenger, or now the teacher, now the student, the child is learning how to act appropriately in many roles. He is learning what it feels like to be in a certain role, and hence is learning about the correlation between feelings and behavior, as well as the consequences of behaving in certain ways. In recent years we have come to realize the value of this kind of play for adults in enhancing their understanding of other people and other roles.

Going back to Groos's definition for a moment, this kind of play does, in one sense, serve a practice function. But it is more a generalized readiness for types of situations that may arise than a rehearsal of specific functions. In other words, the child is learning to be flexible in the face of new situations —he is learning to learn.

Creativity

Play and cognitive development are also related to creativity. Creativity can be seen as one aspect of problem solving, since some solutions are more creative than others. The marks of a creative product are often a matter of dispute (e.g., What makes a great poem?), though there is some consensus that it must be unique and of value to society. There are many problems of definition involved which are beyond the scope of this paper, but we do know something about the characteristics of creative people. They are independent, with a strong need to manipulate the environment in search of solutions.

They are flexible. They play with ideas and hypotheses, however wild, but they are able to impose the discipline of logic and reality on these ideas. Above all, they have an appetite for working on a problem toward a solution. (This is the same problem-solving attitude whose roots are found in play.)

Conclusion

Play is the basis of all higher forms of mental activity, because it serves as a bridge between sensorimotor intelligence and operational thought. In his play, the child progresses from ritualization of an action to new levels of abstraction which form the basis for all forms of symbolic representation: language, concepts, associations, principles, and theories. Through play, the child learns to understand the world on his own terms and to have some control over it to meet his own cognitive needs. Play is where the intellect, the emotions, and the will join forces to carry the child forward to new levels of coping with his expanding world.

Many teachers of young children have long understood the intellectual power of play. What can teachers do when challenged about the value of play for young children? First, they should be prepared to discuss and provide evidence that play does have cognitive value. Second, they should not allow highly structured activities and rigid discipline to infiltrate early childhood programs and usurp the time which should be used in the valuable learning experiences of play.

Above all, the teacher needs to think through the kind of environment she might provide and her role in it. Having ensured that many basic materials for spontaneous play have been provided should she limit herself to observing, answering questions, intervening in disputes or in situations where the child's safety is in question? Or should she be structuring the play activities in such a way as to lead to the development of specific and basic concepts? What is the proper balance between spontaneous, child-centered play and structured, adult-directed play?

In examining Piaget's theory, we must conclude that spontaneous play should predominate. The child must take in reality in his own egocentric way before he can cope with the system of adult logical thought. This places on the teacher the task of judging through observation the tentative concepts, generalizations, and hypotheses of every individual child (just as Piaget observed the association of hanging and swaying in J.). Some of these judgments may come through listening to children's conversations for ". . . doing things in social collaboration in a group effort . . . leads to a critical frame of mind, where children must communicate with each other. This is an essential factor in intellectual development." (p. 4) But the teacher herself can assume this role of questioner, challenging the child to examine the adequacy of his own thinking. She may set up the situation in such a way as to provoke cognitive conflict by demonstrating the unexpected consequences of some line of reasoning. She can suggest ways for the child to test his hypotheses to determine their validity under different conditions.

The teacher is a contributor in no small measure in the child's spontaneous play, not in a heavy-handed manner, but as a fellow problem solver, sharing in both questions and answers. By her own curiosity and interest in investigation she provides a powerful model for the young learner. She knows how and when to provide new stimulation which will move the child to expand or clarify his learning and when to allow time for incubation and assimilation of the old. Such sensitivity and finesse is what makes a creative teacher.

We have lived through the era of the cognitive curriculum in which capitalization on the early learning years was equated with verbal learning of concepts through repetitive drill. Now there is a school of thought which advocates spending the primary school years in developing skills proficiencies, for locating, using, and extending information, and for developing motivational systems which will predispose the child to engage in learning and problem solving of his own volition.

It is important to note that these components are content-free, that is, the kinds of information and problems and learning referred to encompass social, emotional, personal, and practical, as well as intellectual domains.

Rohwer, an educational psychologist who advanced this notion in 1971, believes that once these skills are firmly established, content learning will proceed much more rapidly. It is therefore appropriate, in his view, to postpone such learning to adolescence. The question of curriculum then becomes not when learning should begin, but the kind of learning appropriate for each stage of childhood. In this framework, play comes into its own as a powerful medium for learning during the preschool and elementary school years.

References

Bower, T. G. R. "The Visual World of Infants." *Scientific American* 215, no. 6 (1966): 80-92.

Bower, T. G. R. "The Object in the World of the Infant." *Scientific American* 225, no. 4 (1971): 30-32.

Coleman, J. S. et al. *Equality of Educational Opportunity.* National Center for Educational Statistics, Department of Health, Education, and Welfare. OE-38001, 1966.

Elkind, D. "Piaget and Science Education," *Science and Children* 10, no. 3 (1972): 9-12.

Frank, L. "Play is Valid." *Childhood Education* 44, no. 7 (March 1968): 433-440.

Gagné, R. *The Conditions of Learning,* (2nd. ed.) New York: Holt, Rinehart & Winston, 1970.

Groos, K. *The Play of Man.* New York: Appleton, 1916.

Isaacs, S. *Intellectual Growth in Young Children,* New York: Schocken Books, 1966.

Kagan, J. Speech delivered at the annual conference of the National Association for the Education of Young Children. New York, 1968.

Piaget, J. *Play, Dreams, and Imitation.* New York: Norton, 1962.

Rohwer, W. "Prime Time for Education: Early Childhood or Adolescence?" *Harvard Educational Review* 41 (Aug. 1971).

Additional References on Play

Almy, M. "Spontaneous Play: An Avenue for Intellectual Development." *Young Children* 22, no. 5 (May 1967): 265-277.

Bettelheim, B. "Play and Education." *School Review* 81 (November 1972): 1-13.

Caplan, F., and Caplan, T. *The Power of Play.* New York: Anchor Press, 1973.

Cass, J. *The Significance of Children's Play.* London: Batsford, 1971.

Fowler, W. "On the Value of Both Play and Structure in Early Education." *Young Children* 27, no. 1 (October 1971): 24-36.

Hartley, R. E. *Understanding Children's Play.* New York: Columbia University Press, 1952.

Isaacs, N. "Piaget's Work and Progressive Education." London: National Froebel Foundation, 1965.

Linder, R. *The Fifty-Minute Hour.* New York: Bantam Books, 1954.

Millar, S. *The Psychology of Play.* Baltimore: Penguin, 1968.

Piers, M. W., ed. *Play and Development.* New York: Norton, 1972.

Sutton-Smith, B. "Spontaneous Play: An Avenue for Intellectual Development." *Bulletin of the Institute of Child Study* (University of Toronto), Vol. 28, no. 2, 1966.

Sutton-Smith, B. "The Role of Play in Cognitive Development." *Young Children* 22, no. 6 (September 1967): 361-370.

Sutton-Smith, B. *The Folkgames of Children.* Austin: University of Texas Press, 1972.

Many times, when we observe children at play, we can see ways they are using their play to explore their world, to gain physical and social knowledge, and to solve problems. The difficulty and complexity of the problem to be solved may vary with the age of the child and the nature of the play activity. In most of the following examples of problem solving through play, a crucial element is present which Dewey (1938) feels to be the essential first step in learning the method of inquiry or problem solving—identifying the problem. According to Dewey, knowing how to find a meaningful problem (rather than having someone give you a problem) is the mark of a good problem solver or inquiring scientist, and the learning which occurs through the process is an important part of learning the method of inquiry.

Problem Solving

R., a child of twenty months, sat down to play alone with a set of plastic cups with tops. These cups were of all sizes and each size was in a different color. All the tops were white. The object of the activity is to fit the tops to the cups and then fit each closed cup into the next bigger size cup.

R. would sometimes forget to close a cup with a top and then find herself with too many white tops left over. Sometimes she would fit a cup into one that wasn't the next in size and then she would be left with too many cups and no place where they could fit unless she undid what she had just done.

Through the activity she experienced colors, sizes, coordinating materials (cups and tops that fit together), and the problem-solving process of trial and error.

—◦—◦—

A three-year-old boy was playing alone. He had four pieces of Tinkertoys—two round ones with holes in them and two sticks, one short and one long. He placed the round ones on opposite ends of the long stick and then put the short stick into one of the round ones. He moved this object around in the air, talked to it, and moved it along the floor. Then he moved the short piece to another side of the round one. He called the object a bird. He moved it around and talked to it. He tried to put it in his shoe, but it wouldn't fit, so he took it apart and placed each piece in the shoe. He then took the pieces out of his shoe and put them together again, with the two round pieces in the middle. It kept falling apart, so he tried to push it back together to hold better. He moved it around for awhile, then he had to stop because it was time for him to go to bed. The entire activity lasted about 10 or 15 minutes.

—◦—◦—

A little girl, age three, quickly loaded her wagon with just as many blocks as she could. As she pulled the wagon through a door, blocks fell in every direction. Without annoyance or concern she pushed the wagon through the door again and repeated the process. But this time, with an empty wagon, she stopped and looked. She rolled the empty wagon in and out the door. She had no difficulty. Then she rolled the wagon back in again and loaded it carefully. Not one block extended beyond the edge of the wagon. She pulled the wagon through the door without losing a single block. She not only learned about size in connection with the blocks, door, and wagon but was learning to solve problems.

D., four years old, was observed at play in the kindergarten classroom. Through the use of an ordinary paper cup and a yard of yarn he was capable of creating a great variety of play uses. At first he poked a hole on the back side of the cup and threaded the yarn through the hole and taped it shut. Then he used it as a "telephone," carrying on a conversation with another classmate for several minutes. After the other playmate found something else to do, D. found that the "telephone" could easily be converted into a "microphone" by tying one end of the paper cup to a door knob. At this time he was observed singing, dancing, and talking.

The thing that impressed me the most was the imaginativeness of his play.

A group of four boys play together frequently. One of the boys is in kindergarten, two are in first grade, and one in second. They play outside almost every afternoon, frequently riding bicycles. They are quite adept at riding and have been trying stunts, like standing on one wheel. While I was outside they parked their bikes by our neighbor's garage and went inside. After a short time they reappeared, one carrying two pieces of plywood, about one foot by two feet, and the others carrying bricks. They used the bricks to build a low structure, two bricks wide and two bricks high. They then placed the plywood leading down on each side of the bricks in two ramps. They then began riding bikes up and over the ramp, with the second grader leading. (The ramp was on his sidewalk and the materials used were his.) At first they proceeded cautiously and slowly, then after repeated times with more abandon. After about 15 minutes, they removed one ramp and using just the one incline, began to ride the bikes up the ramp and jump off. Laughter and shouts followed. They also called to each other to watch what they seemed to consider particularly good jumps. The activity continued throughout the afternoon and for the rest of the week.

A group of three five-year-olds were building a block construction with wooden domino blocks, 4"x6". They took turns putting two standing up for the base, and one flat across the top. They continued to build the structure until it reached about 2½ feet high. Then it collapsed.

They began to build it again in the same fashion. Two of the children were doing most of the building, the third child observed and gave his approval of the additions. This time the blocks reached higher than the children's heads, but they continued to reach up and add more. When they got to a point where they had to stand on tip-toe to add more, the last one they put on made the structure collapse.

They rebuilt it again, and the next time it reached above their heads, one of the boys said, "Wait a minute," and went over to get a chair. He stood on it and carefully put more blocks on until it reached higher than his head when he stood on the chair.

Reference

Dewey, J. *Logic, The Theory of Inquiry.* New York: H. Holt and Co., 1938.

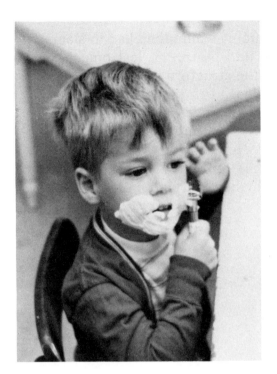

Nancy E. Curry
University of Pittsburgh

Dramatic Play as a Curricular Tool[1]

My experience with young children has convinced me that play is a multipurpose tool which, among other things, assists the child in realizing his effectiveness as the initiator in the learning process. Like many teachers, however, I felt inarticulate about the specific gains inherent in a play curriculum. This discussion has been undertaken with the hope of clarifying the ways in which play contributes to the child's growing sense of mastery as a thinking and feeling person, effective in and on the environment.

RATIONALE FOR A PLAY CURRICULUM

Nature of the Young Child

What the young child brings to the educative process upon entrance into an early childhood program is an abounding sense of curiosity, an intense craving to explore the environment, and if the culture has nurtured it, a predisposition to sym-

---

[1] Based in part upon Chapter V of the unpublished doctoral dissertation, "Current Issues in Play: Theoretical and Practical Considerations for Its Use as a Curricular Tool in the Preschool," University of Pittsburgh, 1972.

bolize thought and fantasies in dramatic play. The young child tends to use fantasy in an integrative way, according to Ruth Griffith, an early psychoanalytically-oriented educator, "As fantasy is the manner of thinking natural in childhood, so is play the child's characteristic mode of behavior." (Griffith 1935, p. 319.)

If you look closely at the development of role play at different ages, you can observe the process by which the child seeks out stimulation, integrates it into already existing structures, and transforms it into novel combinations which are then externalized in symbolic role play. To illustrate, let us contrast the school play of two age groups—three-year-olds and four-year-olds. In a videotape of children's play* the imitative role play of the three-year-old is illustrated when two little girls enact in turn the roles of mother and baby. The play has a docile domestic flavor in which the "mother" puts the "baby" to bed, gives her a teddy bear, and covers her in the toy cradle. In the morning the "baby" is taken to school, which is represented by a chair. Then she is brought home and put to bed again. This play episode is then repeated almost exactly, except that the girls switch roles. These activities are familiar to both children, and in their play are simple and unelaborated. The theme involves loosely developed familial activities in which the whole person (mother, school girl, baby) is represented by a part or single aspect of his appearance or behavior (e.g., sitting on a chair represents school, wearing a hat and carrying a purse represents mother).

In the same videotape the family and school play of the four-year-old is highly elaborated with a pretend bus ride including props such as lunch

* Call No. 911B714, Hillman Library, University of Pittsburgh.

60

boxes and books. The four-year-old mother and baby play centered around going to bed is also greatly differentiated in comparison with that of the three-year-olds. The beginning of the play is highly imitative with careful eye to all necessary details; beds with covers have to be available for all the "babies," as do stuffed toys and baby bottles. The "mother" kisses all of her demanding babies good night and then settles down to do her ironing. The process of getting ready for bed takes much longer at four than it did for the three-year-olds because their broader perceptual horizons dictate an insistence on the faithful representation of a familiar, real-life experience. However, into this play is introduced the novel and scary element of a "ghost" whose howls waken and terrify the babies. The play reaches a fever pitch of excitement which the mother quells, only to have the episode repeated. After the second repetition the ghost becomes the babies' brother who first goes to the store for cigarettes for "mother" and then takes one of his baby sisters to New York.

In this manner, the imitative role play of the three-year-old has changed by the age of four to incorporate many more elements, just as the ideation processes of the child move from the simple juxtaposition ideas to formation of idea sequences (Biber and Franklin 1968, p. 15A). The earlier, more primitive kind of repetitive, imitative play provides the child with the opportunity to consolidate experiences, which form the basis for a varied repertoire of responses from which to draw at a later time.

The contrast between the imitative role play of the three-year-olds with the "scenario" of the four-year-olds illustrates Sutton-Smith's concept of the transformational component of play (Sutton-Smith

1971b). The children begin their play with imitations of perceived adult and child activities. But at age four, the introduction of the ghost seems to be the point at which play is transformed from imitation to novel combinations which broaden the child's conceptual horizons and permit the exercise of autonomy and creativity.

The contrast between the play of two age groups just one year apart illustrates the tremendous cognitive growth that takes place in one year. Further contrasting illustrations of the growth of role play from ages two to ten are now available on films which demonstrate the increasing elaborations in play as the child grows older. (Arnaud and Curry 1973). That children have the capacity for such growth and that opportunities to practice dramatic role playing may enhance cognitive growth present two strong arguments for using a play curriculum.

A preschool curriculum building on the intense desire of the child to act out and personify his perceived world should create an educational framework which has intrinsic value to the child. Because of the egocentric nature of the three-year-old, for example, and his sturdy sense of autonomy, a curriculum imposed from without has little relevance.

Value of Dramatic Play

The literature clearly indicates that the young of all species play, and that the higher on the phylogenetic scale, the more the young of that species play (Arnaud and Curry, unpublished paper). These facts would suggest that play serves some valuable function for the preservation of the species. The presence of symbolic dramatic play as the primary mode of young children in cultures which depend upon the use of complex abstractions speaks of its function in preparing children who are to live in a society in which the ability to handle abstract symbols is essential.

The problem-solving potential of dramatic play is frequently mentioned in the literature. Once a child is caught up in a dramatic role, he will usually go to great lengths to keep the play ongoing. By using Smilansky's (1968, p. 72) framework for the way in which the child organizes play behavior, one can analyze a common play episode (e.g., spaceman play) for its problem-solving qualities: First the child selectively chooses from the environment that to which he will respond (spaceman). Next he spontaneously produces a response that is clearly his own ("Pretend this is our spaceship."). After he expresses his response, others in his environment accept it ("Let's take the ship to the moon!"). Then he takes new cues from the responses of the other children ("Look! There's a moon crater with footsteps in it!"). Using these new cues he selectively forms new responses which continue the play ("Let's call Mission Control to find out what to do.").

Introducing props and exciting ideas help the child bind other players to his idea; to do this successfully, the child must continually surmount social and physical problems, while at the same time contributing zest to the ongoing play.

In today's highly complicated and technological society, it will be essential for our children to develop complex, yet flexible, learning strategies if they are to live as contributing members of a symbolic society. Dramatic play seems to be one vehicle well suited for the development of these learning strategies. Dramatic play involves the ability to understand and abstract the salient features of another's role and requires the capacity for a certain amount of objectivity and empathy, both of which imply that the child is at least practicing the operation of reversibility essential in the cognitive structures described by Piaget (1962).

Further, dramatic play requires the child to move beyond an egocentric position. If he wants others to be able to follow his play ideas, the child must establish sequential temporal landmarks in his play. This involves being able to see things from another person's viewpoint. The ability to keep tuned in on the play involves the ability to focus attention, which also necessitates amending his egocentric point of view. All of these abilities are essential for later success with more abstract learning experiences.

IMPLEMENTATION OF A PLAY CURRICULUM

Environment

The ecology of the traditional nursery school from its beginnings in the mid-nineteenth century has been based on the importance of play. The earliest early childhood centers paid close attention to the selection of equipment which was modeled after adult counterparts (stoves, tables and chairs, boats, farm machinery), simpler versions of actual adult work items (carpentry benches, sewing cards), self-correcting manipulative devices (Froebel and Montessori equipment), climbing equipment for the development of the large muscles, and unstructured media which the child would use to reconstruct his perceived world or to create something new (blocks, clay, paint).

Whether by intuition or with educational intent, teachers chose such equipment to create a world in which children could carry out activities suitable for the expression of their natural mode of behavior, play. All of the aforementioned equipment had the effect of facilitating children's success in their first educational venture outside the home.

Most of the current preschools based on the traditional mode have continued to use similar basic equipment, but with a clearer rationale. This rationale has been refined because the use of such equipment, which has stood the test of time for one group of professionals, may be questioned by another group, such as those favoring more academic preschools. It is very likely that the use of such equipment would become (and, in fact, has been) stereotyped in the hands of complacent, nonintrospective teachers. For example, one might find the standard children's housekeeping equipment (refrigerator, stove, and sink) arranged in an antiseptic school building on a Navaho or Hopi Indian reservation where much of the baking is still done in outdoor clay ovens and where water is drawn from a communal source.

Currently, then, early childhood teachers need to be aware of the importance of creating a play environment in which, as Millie Almy describes,

> . . . there is plenty of cognitive information for the children to accommodate to and at the same time, there is adequate provision for assimilation, that is, for play, which gives the child the opportunity to do his own structuring. (Cited in Curry 1972, p. 136.)

Trips, stories, family-type experiences with the group, as well as recognition of those which have occurred in the child's real family, provide information for the child to accommodate to in the preschool. Toys which are models of some elements of such experiences or "real" objects encourage the playing out and assimilation of these experiences.

In his work, Hunt (1964) has talked of the importance of matching new and old information through the child's interaction with his environment. In these environmental interactions, Hunt feels that the child takes in information which he tests against already coded and stored information acquired through prior environmental encounters. If the new information is too similar to that previously coded and stored, the child becomes bored. If the new information is too alien or at variance with already assimilated information, the child may withdraw. However, when the novel information is neither too foreign nor too well known, a good match is achieved and the child can assimilate it.

The development of a learning situation in which environmental encounters are planned, moderated, and modified by the teaching staff is one of the major tasks of preschool educators. The use of equipment which represents familiar home activities or models of familiar environmental objects provides the child with a safe experiential baseline. From this familiar baseline, the child can make forays into the unknown under the drive for stimulus variation, and can return to this baseline when he finds too much incongruity between what he already knows and the novelty he encounters.

Unstructured materials such as blocks, clay, or paint permit the child to create an environment which is even more congenial than that created by teachers, because it is uniquely his own.

By testing out his capacities for venturing into the unknown, either from the secure environment provided by understanding, knowledgeable adults, or created by himself out of unstructured media, the child begins to develop effective learning strategies.

Role of the Teacher

From the work of Piaget (1962), we know that in the intellectual development of the very young child, sensorimotor activities serve as the predominant mode for interaction with the environment, but that as the child grows older, he switches to more symbolic modes.

The facilitation of the movement from the sensori-motor mode to the symbolic mode may be one of the key functions of the early childhood teacher. Further, this shift from the sensorimotor to the symbolic mode can be clearly seen in dramatic play in which the child moves from imitative role play to the dramatization and symbolization of many aspects of his widening world. It would appear that dramatic play may be the vehicle which the teacher can use to facilitate this shift, if the child is unable to accomplish it alone.

Assisting in this transition requires artistry on the part of the teacher. She must accept the child on the level of development at which he is functioning when he enters nursery school and help him move forward from that baseline. She must resist the temptation to set arbitrary standards which all children are expected to meet, thereby preordaining certain children to be failures as soon as they start school.

The three-year-old entering nursery school needs to be offered play opportunities which allow for a sensorimotor approach to life. It is the role of the teacher at this point to provide items which stimulate, but do not overwhelm, all the sensory modalities (sight, touch, taste, smell, sound, kinesthesia) and to provide opportunities for channeling the direct motor discharge of these sense impressions.

Early precursors of dramatic play can be nurtured by the teacher who builds on the tendency of the young three-year-old to act out sensory impressions on the spot. Permitting the children to watch a plumber repair a sink can be followed by pointing out the tools which are available for the children to use. By highlighting the potential play use of equipment, the teacher indicates to the child that symbolizing experiences in play is an expected and desired activity.

Many opportunities to practice newly acquired skills are needed by the three-year-old; the process of performing an activity provides more pleasure and receives more investment than does the product. This process orientation to play activities is congruent with the sensorimotor nature of the three-year-old's intellectual development, and it is also reflected in the development of his or her dramatic play ability. For example, the early imitative role play seems to be based on the sensory data which the child reproduces in symbolic motor responses.

The major part of the dramatic play of the three-year-old involves the child's acting out a direct replication of a perceived ability of someone admired. The teacher reinforces this play by having available props which are models of familiar elements from the child's environment. Rudimentary role play may be triggered by these props which may represent just one aspect of an admired person's role (e.g., putting on man's hat may render the child "Daddy" for the moment, and he may then engage in activities such as pretending to drive a car).

With practice and adult support, the three-year-old refines and sustains his or her imitative role play to the point that it becomes quite repetitious to the viewer, but highly enjoyable to the participant, as is evident in the videotapes of the three-year-olds mentioned earlier. In this fairly stereotyped role play, we see further evidence of the child's being enmeshed in the process of play (and thus practicing a newly acquired function) rather than being capable of planning a product, which in the case of dramatic play involves developing a plot with a discernible beginning and end. Recognizing when such repetitive play is normal and indeed necessary, and when it represents a developmental lag, requires diagnostic skill on the part of the teacher.

The switch from the sensorimotor to the symbolic play mode is accomplished so smoothly in most young children that there is no clear transition point. Therefore, the teacher consistently sustains and re-inforces the precursors of, as well as the emerging of, dramatic play. Also, she can build on the child's tendency initially to imitate and later to identify with meaningful people in his life, one of whom the teacher inevitably becomes. There is the common phenomenon of a three-year-old reading by holding the book with the pictures facing away from himself, as he has observed his teacher doing when she reads to the class.

The teacher can provide a model of a playful person to the young child by making certain playful gestures, such as pretending to eat the ubiquitous make-believe birthday cakes that children make at the sandbox. She can provide a model of playfulness by expressing verbal concern about one of the characters in the child's ongoing play ("Did your baby's cold get better yet?").

That dramatic play holds real value for the teacher can be expressed to the children in other ways as well. For example, the teacher can reinforce play episodes by sitting near the players and focusing her attention on their play ("I'll read you a story with the others at storytime. Now I want to see what's happening in the block corner."). She can redirect the wandering player ("I think I hear your baby calling you."). Verbally, she can express her appreciation of a play episode ("You've really had fun at play time, haven't you?").

Once the child becomes capable of sustained, involved dramatic play, the teacher continues to be needed as a facilitator, a referee, a representation of reality, and for cognitive and sensory input. Keeping tuned in on the child's experiences in and out of the group gives the teacher the clue as to what props are needed to encourage the use of dramatic play as well as helping her decide what sort of input will lead to more involved assimilative play. The addition of equipment, stories, field trips to local displays, and pictures not only adds an exciting dimension to the play, but also supplies opportunities to reach higher levels of conceptualization.

Play Training

If, in spite of a concentrated effort on the part of the teacher to reinforce, support, model, and facilitate in-depth dramatic play there are still children who use the sensorimotor mode as their primary play mode, the teacher may need to help move them on to more symbolic modes in order to supply the underpinnings of the operations involved in abstract thinking. Smilansky's work with "disadvantaged" Israeli children (1968) has provided an action-research model in play training. She has now begun to replicate this work in the United States with lower-socioeconomic status American children in Columbus, Ohio.

In Smilansky's training schema, the adult diagnoses which of these elements of sociodramatic play are missing in the child's play behavior:

1. Imitative role play
2. Make-believe in regard to objects
3. Make-believe in regard to actions and situations
4. Persistence
5. Interaction between two or more players
6. Verbal communication

Then the adult helps the child develop whatever element is absent from his or her play. In one form of intervention, the teacher actively takes part in the dramatic play of the children by enacting a dramatic role which fits into the ongoing theme of the children's play (being the grandmother who takes the children to the store).

The second form of intervention delineated by Smilansky is an intervention from outside the play in which the adult addresses suggestions, questions, and clarifications to the role of the person the child is depicting, rather than to the child himself ("Doctor, what can you do to fix my broken arm?").

In both of these forms of intervention, the adult models for the child a personified symbolic role. In trying out the Smilansky technique with a small group of nonplaying kindergarteners, I found that the children only needed the adult's participation for a short time before I could move out of the play and the child could carry on dramatizations at a higher level than before.

Marshall and Hahn (1967) found that if an adult engaged in fantasy play with a child, and in the play training acted out roles commonly used by children in dramatic play, the child's dramatic play increased in frequency.

It would appear, then, that children can be trained to develop dramatic play ability. Sutton-Smith (1971a) pointed out that children who seem most easily influenced by such training are children who have had precursor-type play experiences within the family where fantasy is encouraged even in very young children. "It is the social games with the baby in the first eighteen months that 'set the kid up' so he already knows about these incongruous interaction systems." (Cited in Curry 1972, p. 144.)

Currently, there is a movement in early childhood

education to provide many kinds of stimulating experiences for infants. Adults are being taught to play with their infants by using various objects with the goal of providing sensory stimulation. Such projects operate on the premise that early stimulus deprivation may be irreversible so that sending a child to a group program at age three or four may be too late to remediate very early lacks.

Smilansky and Sutton-Smith have concluded from their research projects that the playfulness of young children depends on the modeling provided by the adults in their environment. If this is the case, then the training of parents and teachers to be playful models for the very young child seems warranted.

CONCLUSIONS

Dramatic play is a unifying force by which the child's social and physical experiences with the external world are integrated with his internal mental and emotional processes to produce novel transformations which are then projected outward in symbolic form.

In light of the rapidly expanding and changing society for which the family and the schools are presumably preparing children to become productive members, an awesome responsibility faces parents and other educators. For example, specific subject matter may be obsolete even before the child completes his formal schooling. It would appear, then, that an education based on the development of complex, yet flexible, learning strategies may best prepare children to become contributing members of a highly symbolic society. Play, which is the young child's most natural expressive form, appears to be a vehicle well suited for the development of learning such strategies as the ability to develop and maintain a planned sequence of activities, the ability to abstract and embody the salient features of a situation or role, the ability to focus one's attention, and the capacity for objectivity and empathy.

References

Almy, M. Panel discussion at NAEYC Conference, "Play: The Child Strives Toward Self-Realization," March 3, 4, and 5, 1971.

Arnaud, S., and Curry, N. "The Stimulation of Inquiry and Understanding in the Preschool Child," 1972 (unpublished paper).

Arnaud, S., and Curry, N. *Role Enactment in Children's Play—A Developmental Overview.* 16 mm. color sound film, 29 minutes. University of Pittsburgh. Campus Film Distr. Corp., 20 East 4th St., New York, N.Y., 1973.

Biber, B. and Franklin, M. "The Relevance of Developmental and Psychodynamic Concepts to the Education of the Preschool Child." In *Early Childhood Play,* edited by M. Almy. New York: Selected Academic Readings, 1968.

Curry, N. "Current Issues in Play: Theoretical and Practical Considerations for Its Use as a Curricular Tool in the Preschool." Unpublished doctoral dissertation. University of Pittsburgh, 1972.

Griffith, R. *Imagination in Early Childhood.* London: Kagen, Paul, French and Trubner, 1935.

Hunt, J. McV. *Intelligence and Experience.* New York: Ronald Press, 1961.

Marshall, H., and Hahn, S. "Experimental Modification of Dramatic Play." *Journal of Personality and Social Psychology* 5 (1967): 119-121.

Piaget, J. *Play, Dreams and Imitation in Childhood.* New York: W. W. Norton, 1962.

Smilansky, S. *The Effects of Sociodramatic Play on Disadvantaged Preschool Children.* New York: John Wiley, 1968.

(a) Sutton-Smith, B. Panel discussion at NAEYC Conference. "Play: The Child Strives Toward Self-Realization," March 3, 4, and 5, 1971.

(b) Sutton-Smith, B. "The Playful Modes of Knowing." In *Play: The Child Strives Toward Self-Realization,* edited by G. Engstrom. Washington, D.C.: National Association for the Education of Young Children, 1971.

The play of children often reflects the learning of social expectations, attempts to understand culture appropriate behaviors, and struggles to learn to manage emotions. By symbolic enactment of roles, by investing feelings in materials, and by acting and interacting with other children, they can gain mastery over many aspects of themselves and their environment. The developing self-image of children is reflected in play behavior and by careful observation, teachers may gain important insights into the difficulties and triumphs associated with learning the answer to the question "Who am I?"

Developing Self-Concept

One morning S. and her best friend A. were at play with blocks. They made a building with several different rooms and the girls were discussing what was to go in each. "I'll put a boy and a girl in the living room watching TV," said A. "How about a little girl sleeping in the bedroom?" suggested S. The girls were using the small cylindrical blocks as people and placing them carefully in the proper rooms. "A Mother and Father are in the kitchen doing dishes," said A. "Fathers don't do dishes!" S. insisted. "Sometimes my Daddy does," continued A. "If my Mommy is busy or tired she asks him to help and he says yes."

A four-year-old girl was sitting between

a teacher's aide and a boy at lunchtime in a day care center. T. told the aide that she had a dolly. The aide asked her if she played with her doll. The boy spoke up and said, "I play with my doll." T. said, "Just girls play with dollies, not boys." Mrs. H., the aide, asked T. why only little girls could play with dolls. T. said, " 'Cause they's Mommies." The boy said he had a truck he played with at home. T. then said, "I play with trucks too." Mrs. H. asked T. if she played with trucks why couldn't boys play with dolls? T. finished the conversation with, "Girls can play with dolls and trucks, boys can't play with both."

The subject of this observation was a six-year-old boy, R. The teacher had just reprimanded him for not putting away the game he had been playing with. R. half-heartedly threw the pieces back in the box and put the box on the shelf. Then he took out the container with the play dough. Nobody was in the small alcove with the table designated for dough and clay play as R. proceeded to take the dough out of the container. For the next three minutes R. threw the ball of dough as hard as he could against the table. He then started tearing pieces of dough off the large ball and began squeezing it in his clenched fist. This activity lasted about five minutes. R. then put the dough back in a ball and began to roll it flat with the rolling pin. He then took the cookie cutter and cut out five boy figures and put the excess dough aside. He took a small wooden truck and proceeded to drive over the figures he had just created. When this was complete he put the squashed people and the remainder of the dough back into the container.

The teacher suggested L. tell a story about her two dolls, a boy and girl. This is the story as related by L.

"C. and L. are having a race. L. wins. C. (her brother's name) is sad. He's crying. He doesn't want L. to win. Now he'll have to stay home alone with the baby-sitter." The teacher asked, "Where will L. go?" "L. is going to McDonalds for a treat with Mommy and Daddy." Teacher: "Why doesn't C. go?" L.: "Because L. won. She gets the treat." Teacher: "Do you think C. will like that?" L.: "No, but he didn't win." Teacher: "What would happen if C. won?" L.: "He's bigger. Why should he always win?" Teacher: "What happens next?" L.: "We go and have a coke, some french fries, and a hamburger. Well, maybe we'll let C. go but he'll have to be nice to me. But he'll have to sit in the back seat of the car by himself."

Children are just arriving at the center. Three four-year-old children rush to the housekeeping corner and begin to put on the dress-up clothing.

"I'm the father," says P.

"I'll be the mother," says N. putting on a long skirt.

"I'm the auntie," says A.

T., who is two- and one-half, comes into the house carrying her rather dirty blanket.

"You can be the baby," burst P.

"Yeah," says A. getting the stroller, "you can be the baby."

"T. not baby," says T. turning to leave.

"You be the baby," says N.

"No!" yells T., her lips beginning to pout, "T. NOT baby!" She leaves the children.

It is about 2:45 p.m. The four are again in the housekeeping area. One child tells T., who appears tired from the day's activities, to be the baby. "T. baby," she says climbing into the stroller and beginning to suck on the corner of her blanket while the others push her about the room.

A four-year-old girl was playing house in the kitchen. She used the floor as a stove and cooked dinner with various pots and pans from the cupboard. The little girl talked to herself as she went about her tasks of preparing dinner. She sang and wondered if everyone would like the meal. She then served the meal to imaginary friends seated at the kitchen table.

T., four years old, ran over to the dolls, took one and put her into a high chair. She then began talking to her baby as she proceeded to warm a bottle in a pan over the stove. A second girl came over to the play area and watched silently. Meanwhile, T. took the bottle and fed the doll in her arms while rocking and singing. The second girl then asked if she could play too. T. said, "Sure. You can be my friend coming to visit me." Without question the child sat down near T. and seemed to wait for T. to start her role. T. then began asking, "Do you want some coffee? How are your children?" The little girl began answering the questions, then said, "This is no fun. I want a baby too." She then picked up another doll, took her to a rug outside the play-house area, and undressed and dressed her. T. asked the girl to come back and play, but hearing a negative reply, she put the doll in the cradle and started to iron. A third girl came and started to set the table. T. asked her if she wanted to play house with her. The new girl said, "No." T. stood and watched her finish setting the table, and then left the play area and worked on a puzzle.

The boys had been playing football for a long time. They were approached by one girl about eight years old who asked to play with them. She was told "no" by one of the boys very distinctly. She then asked again in a few moments and was again told "no" by the same boy. Another boy about his same age and build then said, "Ah come on, what are you, a male chauvinist?" "No," replied the other boy, "only when it comes to baseball." The girl was not allowed into the game.

A three-year-old boy spent approximately 15 to 20 minutes of free play period moving the housekeeping furniture in different positions. He moved the stove, sink, cupboard, and doll bed into another area and then back to the housekeeping area in the new positions. He involved two other boys in this activity. Those two boys only followed his lead in the process of moving the equipment. After everything was relocated P. lay down the doll bed and said, "There now, I am in my new house and I can sleep better." He repeated similar variations of this play for two weeks.

Doris Sponseller
Oakland University

Matthew Lowry
Formerly of Oakland University

Designing a Play Environment for Toddlers

Play as a prevalent type of behavior in young children has long been recognized by educators, psychologists, and laymen alike. Whether play behavior should be examined as a subject worthy of independent structural analysis, or as a means to serve some other function, or even whether it should be explained away completely by other constructs has been a source of disagreement (Herron and Sutton-Smith, 1971). It is our belief that children's play deserves serious study and we are supportive of the increasing emphasis it is again receiving.

Our specific area of interest is the spontaneous play of the child of toddler age—approximately 14 to 30 months—in the context of a group setting. Since we have designed an environment for toddlers it is important for us to determine whether this environment is an optimal one for facilitating spontaneous play.

Play in infants and toddlers has not been a prime focus of observation except for records of individual children in their home environments. Although this information is not extensive, knowledge of toddler play behavior in a group environment is even more limited, primarily because group facilities for toddlers are few in number. Major research on the play of groups of young children, from the early work of

Parten (1932) up to the more recent work of Smilansky (1968) have been with children older than age two. Therefore we do not really know whether the spontaneous group play behaviors observed by these researchers in three-, four-, and five-year-old children are also evident in groups of toddlers.

The study of individual children's play has been of two types. Play behaviors in the young child of three to five have been studied by experimental methods. For example, the work of Hutt (1966) attempts to differentiate exploration ("What does this object do?") from play ("What can I do with this object?") by exposing children to a novel object and categorizing the child responses. Experimental studies of play have rarely focused on children of the toddler age range, however. What we know presently of types of toddler play behavior comes primarily from the observation studies of the individual child at home. Investigation is needed to determine whether the types of toddlers' play behavior exhibited in the home carry over to the group setting. Therefore, as a focus of our work, we have attempted to observe spontaneous toddler play using categories developed by those who have described either individual toddler play or group play of older preschoolers.

One of the major contributors to cataloging individual infant and toddler play is Piaget (1962) who observed his own children during these years and extensively described their early practice play, motor games, and beginnings of symbolic play. Piaget categorizes play as assimilation, in contrast to imitation, which he sees as accommodation to reality. In practice, however, it is often difficult with toddlers to differentiate imitative play from play and from imitation.

The same problem occurs with the theoretical

framework of Hutt. In toddlers, exploring and play are so closely intertwined that exploratory play may be a more appropriate name for much of their activity. Using Parten's continuum of categories for social play ranging from onlooking through solitary, parallel, associative, and cooperative play, we have found that in toddlers onlooking is often a group behavior rather than an individual behavior. That is, a novel event, object, or noise will cause the children to collect in "herds" or to travel in a group to see what is of interest. We have termed this behavior "herding" or "group onlooking."

Thus, the categorization of toddler play, according to any one previously developed theoretical framework, is often difficult.

A method for categorizing toddler play

Our interest in designing a method for categorizing toddler play has come from two sources: the practical problems encountered in attempts to design an environment suitable for toddlers; and the theoretical basis from which our program operates (James et al. 1972).

The philosophy of the Oakland University Toddler Program is basically Piagetian. We believe a child's development may be attributed to the four interrelated processes discussed in Piaget's work.

These processes are:

1. maturation (the child's physiological growth)

2. social interaction (the child's experiences with people)

3. physical interaction (the child's interactions with things)

4. equilibration (the child's efforts to or-

ganize and to relate all of his/her experiences mentally)

Since maturation and equilibration are relatively free from the influence of outside forces, our major emphasis was placed on the development of appropriate social and physical environments.

We have focused on three areas. First, anecdotal records and ethological running accounts have indicated some of the major characteristics of toddler play. Secondly, we have designed a physical environment which we feel will facilitate the development of wide ranging, increasingly complex, and increasingly social play behaviors. Now we are beginning to systematically observe and organize the specific play behaviors which occur in this environment according to a schematic model which utilizes the play categories of Piaget and the dimensions of social play discussed by Parten.

Before describing the model, however, we will address the first two concerns: the characteristics of toddler play and the design of the physical environment which best facilitates this play.

CHARACTERISTICS OF TODDLER SPONTANEOUS PLAY

▶ Practice Play

Most of the spontaneous play behaviors common among the toddlers in the Oakland University center are sensorimotor or exploratory types, which we are including in the practice play category. These can be both gross and fine motor activities. Some examples are the following:

Primarily gross motor practice play

1. Body movement such as walking or

running: Much of toddler exploratory or practice play is related to their own motor activity. Because they have just recently acquired mobility they enjoy playing with movement. For example, toddlers may be observed playing with walking—on their toes, backward, with the beat of their own music, on blocks, with a limp, with a stoop at every step, and with a variety of speeds.

2. Climbing up: Toddlers climb because something is there, even though adults do not always consider as climbing equipment all of the objects toddlers do. Chairs, tables, people, and toys have all been used for climbing.

3. Climbing in: Toddlers enjoy climbing into things. They may not completely fit, such as climbing into a dish pan, or they may be swallowed up by climbing into a cupboard. It does not seem to matter about the size of the child in relation to the container. As long as part of the child fits, it is a successful experience.

Combined gross and fine motor practice play

1. Gathering: Most toddlers spend time each day collecting materials—large or small. This may serve as an end in itself or may be combined with other play behaviors.

2. Filling: Toddlers can spend a good portion of the day filling containers with continuous substances like water or

discontinuous objects like beads. Many containers, including cups and pans, pockets, wagons, or barrels can be used for the filling play.

3. Dumping: That which is gathered and filled can also be dumped. However, dumping does not necessarily follow filling. Often dumping is done extensively by a child as an activity in itself.

4. Stacking: This is a form of gathering which involves a primitive ordering quality.

5. Knocking down: This behavior is related to stacking as dumping is to filling. Often stacking seems to be done primarily so that knocking down can occur.

Primarily fine motor practice play

1. Trial and error manipulation: Toddlers enjoy tiny toys, puzzle pieces, and other small objects which can be held, fitted together, or even taken home in a pocket.

2. Sensory exploration: This behavior appears in many areas of the child's world. It may take place outside with mud, or at the dinner table with mashed potatoes or ice cream. The child may explore with finger paint, water play, or sand.

▶ Symbolic Play

Initial types of symbolic play can also be observed in toddlers. This includes play with materials, verbal symbols, and other children.

1. Play with materials: Toddlers indulge in much imitative play using materials. For example, "feeding a baby" with nonexistent food is common toddler play. While it is probably initially imitation, play variations of the imitative act are numerous.

2. Play with verbal symbols: Since the toddler is at the earliest stages of language production, his attempts to master language require a great deal of play with language. Often materials provide the impetus for language play; for example, reading books may initiate a sequence of language play.

3. Play with other children: Symbolic play occurs extensively in the presence of other children. However, there is usually no differentiation of roles. For example, children may be playing house, but no one is the mother or the father (there are occasionally babies—usually the smallest child, or the one who is siting in the high chair). Everyone fixes dinner, everyone eats dinner, everyone sets the table, everyone takes care of the dolls—everyone does everything.

▶ Games With Rules

Toddlers exhibit the beginning stages of being able to participate in games with rules. Although they are usually capable of playing some simple games initiated by adults, they also play games spontaneously. Sometimes these games seem to start as imitative play initiated by adults; however, other primitive games with child-initiated rules can often be observed. These games tend to be very short in duration and are of these general types:

1. Motor games with rules provided by a single child: These are invented by toddlers playing alone. Since the child of toddler age cannot usually explain the rules, it is sometimes difficult for the adult to recognize these rule games. Often the adult first realizes the rule exists when the child cries after the rule has been inadvertently broken by the adult. Practice play frequently follows a rule; for example, the puzzle pieces must be put back in a certain order.

2. Social tag games with rules accepted by two or more children: Toddlers engage in a type of game which often has an element of chase or excitement. They interact together in a taglike manner. Perhaps one chases the other and the chaser becomes the chased according to some rule which both children accept. The reciprocal element is important and the presence of another child enhances and sustains the game.

3. Parading: This is a group activity in which toddlers engage that may be likened to a primitive follow the leader. Children may follow each other on tractors or pulling toys or form other types of parades.

THE PHYSICAL ENVIRONMENT AS A FACILITATOR OF PLAY

Description of the environment

The physical environment of the Oakland University Toddler Program has undergone many changes. These have been primarily due to our growth in expertise for designing such environments for toddlers. This growth has been facilitated by an acquisition of one of the farm buildings of the estate on which our campus is located. This building provided us with the opportunity to design an environment especially for our program, after we had been in operation in another building for six months. We were able to learn from previous mistakes and successes and to begin again when necessary.

The building in which we are now located is approximately 75′ by 25′ and is divided into two main parts (Figure 1). The southern third of the building houses the bathroom (1), the cloakroom (2), the activity room (3), and the family room/office (4). The activity room contains paint easels, a water table, tables for activities, supplies, and three large sinks. It is used with small groups of children for art and sensory activities. The family room/office is an office with a small desk and filing cabinets. It is also a family room, carpeted, with curtains, a couch, stuffed chairs, plants, books, a few toys, and a stove. It is designed to provide children who need some time out of the group setting with a place to be alone, in an attempt to create a more homelike atmosphere at school.

The northern two-thirds of the building houses the largest and most significant part of the physical environment. This area, a large room approximately 50′ long by 25′ wide, is dominated by a structure

Figure 1

Floor Plan of the Toddler Physical Environment

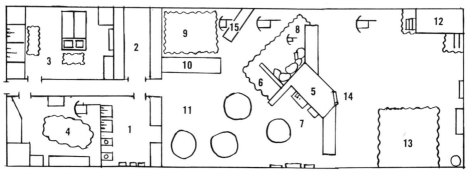

1. Bathroom
2. Cloakroom
3. Activity Room
4. Family Room/Office
5. Octopus
6. Fine Motor Area
7. Home Area
8. Book Area
9. Resting Area
10. Purple Cow
11. Snack/Lunch/Table Area
12. Mountains and Caves
13. Gross Motor Area #2
14. Gross Motor Area #3
15. Green House

Carpeted or Padded Areas

we call the Octopus (5). The Octopus was designed by faculty in Early Childhood Education and the staff of the Toddler Program, and built by the staff and parents of the latter. It represents what we feel is a new concept in environmental planning in early childhood education. The Octopus creates several non-room rooms; provides storage space for equipment and materials being used by the children as well as those which are not in use; and provides for a small but flexible and functional observation facility.

Each of the non-room rooms created by the Octopus represents areas that might be found in other early childhood programs with modifications to make them age appropriate for toddlers. There is a fine motor area (6) with puzzles, pop beads, farm animals, stacking toys, nesting cups, and other manipulative toys. The next non-room is the home area (7), complete with a small stove and sink unit,

table, chairs, a doll bed, high chair and carriage, and items commonly found in a home (dishes, cups, bowls, pans, food cartons, plastic bottles, and dolls). Around the other corner from the fine motor area is the book area (8). In addition to the large collection of books, there are floor pillows and rocking chairs, providing more comfortable locations for children and staff to read books.

Two other areas in the room, only indirectly defined by the Octopus, are the resting corner (9) and the snack/lunch/table area (11). The former provides an area for napping and is found in a corner of the room. It is bounded on a third side by the Purple Cow (10), a large storage cabinet built by the parents. One side of the cabinet provides for the storage of napping supplies and the other serves as the location of the parent's bulletin board. This area is bounded on a fourth side by an additional cabinet, the Green House (15) which provides additional storage space for napping supplies and serves as a science center.

In the adjacent corner is the snack/lunch/table area which is used for eating, as additional space for using fine motor materials, or for doing other activities.

At the far end of the building is the gross motor non-room room (12, 13, 14). This area is divided into smaller subareas. In one corner is Mountains and Caves (12), another piece of equipment designed by the staff. This is a social/climbing piece of equipment. Across the room is a large area (14) which is put to many uses. Sometimes it serves as a spot for the tepee climber; at other times for the large hollow plastic blocks; it has also been the location of the rocking boat, the rocking horses, and the tumbling mats. The remainder of the gross motor area (13) houses the unit blocks, small cars and trucks, the larger trucks, tractors, boats and trailers for riding, pull toys, and most important, space in which to use this equipment.

WAYS THE PHYSICAL ENVIRONMENT FACILITATES PLAY BEHAVIOR

The nature of the child's play behaviors is determined by two factors which are consolidated from Piaget's four (see p. 83) interrelated processes: the child and his/her previous experiences, and the nature of the environment in which the play takes place.

We have little or no control over the first factor except to require that all children enrolled in the program use walking as the primary means of self locomotion. It is beyond the scope of this program to require that the children have had any other experiences.

We do have control over the environment and therefore we have focused our attention upon the environment as it facilitates practice play, symbolic play, and the play of games with rules.

One form of practice play which the environment can influence is gathering. We learned early in our experiences that toddlers gather almost anything that can be collected. Our original environment allowed for some gathering, though we did not plan it that way. We had pop beads, books, puzzles, and blocks which the children could gather. We soon added more of these and some additional gathering materials. These additions included kitchen items, especially saucers, cups, bowls, pans, and empty food containers; wooden people; farm animals; balls; puppets; and shape boxes.

Soon after the toddler begins to gather, he/she seeks a place to put these gatherings. In our first building we had more things to gather than we had places to leave the collections, so the favorite place to leave the gatherings was the center of the room. This made it difficult for the toddlers to walk across the room. Finding a place to lie down on the floor to read a book or work on a puzzle or to play with the blocks became difficult. In addition to discouraging these other behaviors, the gathering play became contagious. At times, every toddler in the room was engaged in gathering behaviors.

This was not unique to our program or to our toddlers. Others who were working with groups of toddlers shared similar problems. Everything came together in the center of the room. We tried to provide containers to serve as additional gathering places, but this solution added to the problem. These containers led to the practice play behavior of dumping, so we were no closer to a solution.

In the planning of the physical environment of the new building, we attempted to eliminate this difficulty. The Octopus is our solution and now occupies the center of the room. Each small area adds to the solution by creating a number of places that are physically separated from sources for gathering. We also have built-in places which serve as areas in which a child may leave his/her gatherings. Many of our cabinets have large open spaces at floor level. When these are not occupied by a tractor and trailer, or a child, one may find a collection, the results of some child's gatherings.

A second area of practice play which the environment facilitates is climbing behavior. We designed and built into our first environment Mountains and Caves, a large piece of climbing equipment. It had places to climb up and slide down; places to climb in, under, and out. The toddlers enjoyed it, and it saw much use as a piece of equipment for climbing.

However, so did the tables, chairs, book shelves, stove, sink units, and heater covers. We soon discovered that until we could provide other possibilities for climbing, the children would climb whatever was available. We attempted to protect the children from falling and to encourage appropriate locations for climbing, knowing that was only a temporary solution.

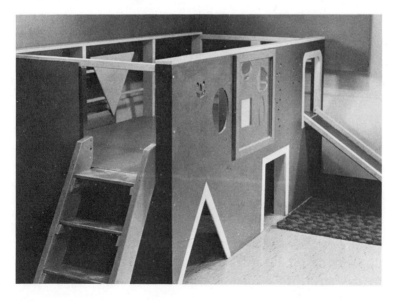

Our new structured physical environment provides more opportunities for appropriate climbing behavior and tends to eliminate many inappropriate behaviors. We constructed our cabinets to make the lowest shelf too high for use as a foothold. The low cabinets mentioned in the discussion of gathering also serve as places to climb inside. We also have space to offer other climbing equipment, like the tepee climber, rocking boat, and hobby horses. These changes in the physical environment have accomplished what we hoped they would. We still have some inappropriate climbing, but it is task oriented —climbing to get something out of storage or off the top of a shelf, rather than climbing for practice.

A third example of practice play which we try to facilitate is that which we call sensory exploration. Using finger paint to cover one's face and arms, or dripping paint brushes on the floor, are examples of this play behavior. The behavior is directed toward discovery of "What can the medium do?" as opposed to "What can I do with the medium?"

In our first environment, we could not provide the children with as many opportunities for this kind of practice play because we were in one room. Toddlers should not be expected to remain with an activity for more than a short length of time. As a result, children entered and left the provided activity constantly. Children were reading books with fingerpainted hands, and painting puzzles, so that staff was spending more time in a police role than in a caregiver role.

Our new building has an activity room with terrazzo floors and a drain in the middle of the room. The walls are ceramic block, and are easily cleaned. This room is used for sensory exploratory activities with small groups of children. No longer are the children limited in their explorations by adult standards. This new physical environment and the resultant new social environment has allowed, in fact encouraged, more practice play in the sensory exploration area.

Symbolic play may also be encouraged by the physical environment. This is particularly true when one carefully selects the kinds of materials for use in the environment. Books, puppets, home items, blocks, wheel toys, and hats are all items found within our environment which encourage symbolic play.

Some people approach books for toddlers with undue caution, banning books from toddlers, insisting that adults be present when the child has a book, or limiting the library to cloth books or cardboard books with heavy pages. Our approach was cautious in the beginning, and we still keep a watchful eye on the books. We found, however, that children soon stop using the books for practice and begin to use books in a more acceptable manner.

Some of our most popular books are what we call success with language books. These books provide a successful experience for the child who is learning to speak since the books usually have the same thing on every page or on every facing page. John Hamburger's Lazy Dog is a good example. On every page, or opposing page, the dog and the ball he is chasing appear. A child soon learns to identify these two items and can "read" the book. Books with abundant pictures of animals or household items also fall into this category if the child is able to recognize an item and name it.

Symbolic play with animal puppets is also popular. We have soft plastic puppets, including two ducks, a whale, a frog, and a wolf. All of these animals, particularly the ducks, are interacted with as if they were hungry. They "nibble" on people's knees, legs, elbows, and arms. The children "feed" the puppets popcorn to appease them. Those controlling the puppets continually seek new sources of food. This play behavior may also be considered as game behavior as there are at times child-initiated rules which must be followed.

Another feeding behavior that is a type of symbolic play occurs in the home area. The food preparation is more elaborate here than with the puppets. Scrambled eggs and muffins are often "cooked" on the stove in pans. Sometimes hot toast, coffee, tea, milk, and juice are also served to those present. At times the activity can be very sophisticated. On the afternoon following a morning snack of blueberry pancakes, one child served another child blueberry pancakes, using the small texture discs for pancakes. The meal included chocolate milk from a chocolate colored plastic bottle and orange juice from an orange one.

This kind of play behavior did not occur in our old building, where home area was much more limited in supplies, space, and facilities. The table was light and easily moved. A child trying to eat at it had to contend with the "move the table game." Everything was too close together, making it difficult to find room in which to play. The additional space, equipment, and facilities in our new building seem to have encouraged more symbolic play.

Hats and other props also play an important part in the symbolic play behaviors of toddlers. They seem to help form the stimuli for play behavior in which the child uses symbols. An example of this may be found with the addition of fire hats to our home area. Soon we began to have firemen, and shortly thereafter, the tractors became fire trucks and the blocks became fire hoses. One child built fire trucks with the hollow blocks, used Mountains and Caves as a fire truck, and put out fires on the tepee climber. The addition of cowboys' hats caused a similar rise in cowboy play behaviors including riding the hollow blocks for horses, and building campfires, although little gun play has been observed. One child, whose father works in the building trades, only builds buildings when he is wearing the hard hat. Carpenter aprons, brief cases, or similar items can also be used to extend children's symbolic play behaviors.

Examples of game behavior have been mentioned earlier in the discussion of symbolic play. Other examples of game behavior and pregame behavior abound. Mountains and Caves is called a social/climbing piece of equipment now because of the possibilities for game behavior the children have found in it. Peek-a-boo is one game which the children frequently play, from around corners, out of its holes, large and small, from underneath to out, and from below to above. The game was so popular that we have built large spaces underneath some of our cabinets to provide additional opportunities for this game.

Finger grab is another game found with Mountains and Caves. Numerous small holes have been drilled on one side. These holes provide the opportunities for one child to stick his/her fingers out or in and a second (or third or fourth child) to grab them or to push them out. Children begin to take turns at this, sometimes sticking in or out, sometimes grabbing or pushing. A variation takes place with the wooden people who just happen to fit in the holes. When pushed out, they fall to the floor, usually bringing a ring of laughter from the children participating.

Ball games from atop, underneath, or below Mountains and Caves are also popular. Some of these games involve rolling the ball down the slide and another child pushing it back up again, all this being accompanied by laughter. Sometimes the game of rolling catch takes place between a child who is underneath and one who is outside. And for the children who can throw the ball up that high, a ball game from up to down and back again may also be found.

Mountains and Caves has always been a part of our environment. We have observed that the addition of other similar items have had similar effects. For example, the construction of the cabinets mentioned earlier has served as a stimulus to game play behavior. So too has the tepee climber, especially in the ball and peek-a-boo games. A large soap barrel in which the children can climb and look out has also led to the peek-a-boo games and some hide-and-seek games, though the latter usually are adult initiated and then imitated by the child later.

A MODEL FOR CATEGORIZING TODDLER PLAY IN THE PHYSICAL ENVIRONMENT

Design of the model

The model is two dimensional, one dimension being the types of play behavior (practice, symbolic, games) and the other being the social quality of the behavior (onlooking, solitary, parallel, associative, cooperative).

The types of play were described in the previous section. The social quality of the play behavior of toddlers 14 to 30 months of age is defined as follows:

> Onlooking—observing, talking, but not participating.
>
> Solitary—play without reference to other children.

Parallel—play of a companionable nature with similar materials but with no personal interaction.

Associative—play which is loosely organized around a common activity, shared interests, and materials.

Cooperative—play with different roles, common goals, usually with one or two leaders, of relatively long duration and complexity.

Cooperative play should not be expected of toddlers.

The model is designed with the types of play behavior in the horizontal axis and the types of social behavior on the vertical axis (Figure 2).

Figure 2

Observation Form

Two-Dimensional Play Model

	Symbolic	Practice	Games
Onlooking			
Solitary			
Parallel			
Associative			
Cooperative			

Initial data on toddler play using the Model

We have now begun the process of gathering observations of the spontaneous play behavior of the toddlers from 14 to 30 months of age in the program and categorizing them according to the model's dimensions. Figure 3 gives examples of the way in which types of play behaviors fit into the model dimensions and these examples are described in detail.

1. A child who is watching the puppets eat popcorn is recorded as having taken the role of an onlooker to symbolic play behavior.

2. The child who builds with one or more children exhibits parallel or associative, practice or symbolic play. Associative play behaviors are exhibited if the children are building together, rather than building independent of one another. The play is recorded as symbolic if a particular structure is being built. Thus, two children building a barn together would be recorded as having exhibited associative symbolic play.

3. Building may also fall within the grouping of game behaviors if it is accompanied by children's rules for building. In one instance of building and knocking down, the latter activity could not take place until all the blocks had been used. The child who violated this rule was verbally reprimanded by others in the group. This play behavior would be classified as associative game play.

4. Practice play behaviors often occur in conjunction with walking. A child who

Figure 3

Observation Form: Examples

Two-Dimensional Play Model

	Symbolic	Practice	Games
Onlooking	(1) observing duck puppets eating popcorn		
Solitary	(7) animal puzzle; animals talk	(4) walking on pillows	(8) blocks—putting away
Parallel	(6) cooking pig	(9) painting	
Associative	(2) building barn together	(5) rolling on pillows	(3) building, knocking down—rule
Cooperative			

Child_____

Age_____

Date_____

Observer_____

spends much time walking on pillows (as opposed to walking over them to get from point A to point B) is recorded as having exhibited a practice play behavior. If this is done alone, it is recorded as solitary practice play.

5. A similar practice play behavior is exhibited by the children who roll on the pillows together. This behavior seldom remains solitary for very long, as it usually attracts more children. The play behavior is characterized by interactions between the children, as one child's behavior stimulates another. Thus, one child's giggles stimulates another's; falling by one stimulates the same behavior in the other children. This play behavior would be classified as associative practice play.

6. Parallel play occurs when the children play alongside one another, use similar materials, but have little or no contact with one another. Two children cooking in the home area could exhibit such play behaviors. One toddler was observed cooking a plastic pig in a pan on a stove. Such behavior would be recorded as symbolic. As a second child was also cooking in the home area, but not with the first, the pig cooking play behavior was classified as parallel symbolic play.

7. Many of the animals found in the toddler program are involved in symbolic play behaviors. One such set of animals is that found in a simple four piece

puzzle. One child was observed using the puzzle pieces as animals, walking them on the carpet, and having them make the appropriate animal noises. As this child was playing alone, the play behavior was recorded as solitary symbolic play.

8. This same child was later observed putting the unit blocks away. The non-rectangular shaped blocks are kept in a plastic dish pan. The rectangular blocks are stacked in two groups on the shelf. The large pressed wood roofs are kept under or next to the dish pan. This child was engaged in putting each block in its correct place. The dish pan was searched and re-searched to make certain that blocks which did not belong were put in the appropriate places. As the child was playing alone, the behavior was recorded as solitary play. As the play behavior had rules, it was also recorded as game behavior.

9. The activity room is one area in which much parallel play is found. A group of children painting at the table are working near one another, but not painting together. Sometimes their behaviors are similar, as in the case of some sensory exploration play behaviors mentioned earlier, but the activity is still performed by each of the children individually within the group. Such an activity would be classified as parallel practice play.

The observational method is that of time sampling at 30-second intervals. An individual child's play behavior is recorded for 12 minutes (24 observations). Pilot data was obtained for 864 observations. The percentage of play which fell into each category is indicated on Figure 4. One finding of interest was that the level of spontaneous associative play (22.78 percent) was almost equal to the level of parallel play (25.57 percent). As was expected, however, solitary play is still the predominant type in our sample of toddlers (37.55 percent). Similarly, although practice play was predominant (56.16 percent), the level of symbolic play was high (35.91 percent). Although spontaneous games were less than 10 percent of the total, this study indicates that toddlers in our sample did spontaneously engage in games with rules.

Figure 4

Percentages of observed play in each category

Two-Dimensional Play Model	Symbolic	Practice	Games	Quality of Social Behavior TOTALS
Onlooking	3.72	8.48	1.74	13.94
Solitary	12.90	23.14	1.51	37.55
Parallel	7.67	17.32	.58	25.57
Associative	11.62	7.21	3.95	22.78
Cooperative		.01		.01
Types of Play Behavior TOTALS	35.91	56.16	7.78	

Conclusion

In this chapter, we have outlined some of the major characteristics of toddler play, discussed how the environment facilitates these play behaviors, developed a means for assessing the type and social quality of this play using a two-dimensional model, and provided preliminary data on the frequency of play in each category.

We hope to be able to collect sufficient data so that group toddler play can be compared to group play of older preschoolers and to individual toddler play in the home environment. It is our present hypothesis that one of the major reasons toddlers have exhibited little social play with other children is that they have not had the opportunity to be in a group setting for an extended period. Only further collection of data on their spontaneous play in the Toddler Program environment will be able to determine if this hypothesis is supported.

References

Herron, R. E., and Sutton-Smith, B. *Child's Play*. New York: John Wiley and Sons, 1971.

Hutt, C. "Exploration and Play in Children." *Symposium of the Zoological Society of London*, 18 (1966): 61-81.

James; Lowry; Mayala; McCloy; O'Neill. *Kim: The Initial Report of the Oakland University Toddler Program*, Rochester, Mich.: Early Childhood Project, Oakland University, School of Education, 1972.

Parten, M. B. "Social Participation among Preschool Children." *Journal of Abnormal and Social Psychology*, 33 (1932): 243-269.

Piaget, J. *Play, Dreams and Imitation in Childhood*. New York: W. W. Norton and Company, 1962.

Smilansky, S. *The Effects of Sociodramatic Play on Disadvantaged Preschool Children*, New York: John Wiley and Sons, 1968.

Play by toddlers takes many forms. Practice and symbolic play as well as games with self-imposed rules can be observed. Social interaction occurs with other children and adults. The learning which takes place is self-paced and wide ranging.

Toddler Play

H. is holding and taking apart plastic connecting beads while standing in the household area. H. moves to the table and puts the beads on the table; some fall on the floor. H. sits down on the floor next to a silver lunch box that is already opened, pulls apart the beads, and drops them into both sides of the lunch box one by one. H. then moves to a kneeling position. She gives up trying to close the lunch box and slides over to grab a purse. H. looks at the purse, drops it, and slides back to the lunch box. She starts taking the beads out one by one and drops them on the floor. She stops and tries to close the lunch box, but can not do it so she opens it again and takes out two beads. H. puts them back together, shakes them and puts them on the floor. H. takes two more out of the lunch box and connects them, then takes another one. While trying to attach it, she looks up at people talking in the hallway, but never stops her attempt to connect the third bead. H. finally connects it and places

109

the beads next to the two that she previously put together. She then moves three beads that were already together next to the others. H. stares at the observer while taking out one bead, placing it next to the others in the pattern. Then she takes out another bead and places it in the pattern. H. takes more out while looking at people walking by.

D. is sitting on his tractor in the middle of the block area. He looks at a teacher and B. talking by the house. D. gets another riding tractor and puts the two side by side in the middle of the area near the mats. He rides one a little toward Mountains and Caves and stops. He looks at the girls playing with the house.

D. rides the tractor behind B., going toward the house. He tries to pull the front of the tractor onto the mat. He gets on the tractor again and rides up close to B. and A. He makes sounds to the girls as he looks at them. They ignore him.

D. then rides the tractor toward the middle of the area, stops, and watches a teacher and K. at Mountains and Caves. He backs up in line with the back door, stops, and watches a teacher and K. play peek-a-boo on Mountains and Caves. He rides the tractor over to the rug by the slide end. He gets off the tractor and goes to the steps where K. is climbing. He takes her hand off the side of the ladder, and she gets down. D. climbs up the steps, turns around looking toward center of room, comes down one step, looks around and then sits down. He gets back on the tractor, turns it around, and rides toward the mirror of the observation booth. He comes up very close, stops, puts one hand on the mirror, smiles, pats it once and says, "Me." Then he backs the tractor up and rides into the kitchen area. He turns around and rides back toward the mats.

A group of three children was playing with blocks. C. announced, "I'm goin' in a tunnel this minute! I'm comin'," (with a pull-toy cow). He observed T. approaching, and then loudly exclaimed, "You not playing with my motorcycle." He quickly leaped up, grabbed his cycle which was on the mat, and plopped back down again. C. then stated in a very authoritative manner, "I'm a farmer; give me some milk." The teacher got him some milk. C. gave the cow a drink of milk from the bottle. Suddenly, he yelled, "He won't moo!" The teacher explained, "You're sitting on his cord." He returned to the cow, "Yum, yum." Sometimes gabbing to himself and sometimes to others, he continued, "Want some chocolate milk. Yeh, this one's chocolate milk. Want some hay. What's in your nose?" He examined the cow's nose. He then began modeling other children eating blocks (food). C. joined in saying, "Mine grapefruit. I eat a hamburger. Fried eggs; I eat some of your eggs. Give me some sausage. M., eat some of your eggs. Ow!" He had clunked the block on his nose and threw the block in a pretend waste basket, modeling another child. He then snatched up another block of food and began chewing with grunting and snorting noises. He asked his cow, "Want some of my bite?" C. then laid down on the mat, keeping an eye on his cow. Others tried feeding the cow. "No!" C. shouted, "He had his! Don't put it in his nose!" And suddenly, "Where's my motorcycle?"

M.'s eyes slowly looked up to the teacher as she carefully touched a container of pudding and slid it on the table in front of her. The teacher showed her how to put the pudding onto a cookie sheet where she would use it like finger paint. "Don't help me, wa, wa, wa, wa," she murmured. As she watched the others, she began to scribble and wiggle her fingers in the pudding, mixing two colors together. She scribbled faster, eventually slowly lifting a finger to her mouth and tasting the pudding. She quickly lifted her hands in the air and wiggled her fingers about. Laughingly she said, "You have bumps in yours, bumps." She quickly tasted the pudding again using only one finger. Then she used all four fingers to scrape up the pudding and put it into her mouth. She took long strokes with all four fingers and slowly lifted as much pudding to her mouth as her fingers would hold. Her tongue stuck out of her mouth as she scraped the pan with her fingers. Cheerfully she said, "I'm done."

The teacher, sitting between B. and M., was talking to them about the dough. B. began rolling her piece like a snake. B. stood up by the table smiling and imitated the pounding action of the teacher on the play dough.

B. walked over to the stove and picked

up a purple cup from the burner. She took it back to the table, put the play dough in the cup, and reached with her right hand to get a cylindrical wooden block. B. took the dough out of the purple cup, put it on the block, and began rolling the block.

C. walked by and said, "Where's my fire hat?" B. responded, "I don't know." Then B. made a "pancake" with her dough and put holes in it with a large bobby pin. B. put the pancake in the cup, walked over to the stove, set it on the left burner, and walked back to the table. When the teacher asked if the cupcakes were ready, B. walked back to the stove, opened the oven door, and took the cupcakes back to the table. She commented, "I makin' an oven." She began removing the cupcakes one at a time and reached for more dough.

B. picked up the cupcake tin and walked back to the oven, put the cupcakes inside, and closed the door. Then she sat on the floor in front of the oven. She stood up, turned on the burners, opened the door of the oven and looked inside. She lay down on the floor. She stood up, walked back to the table, picked up a dish with play dough, turned around, placed it in the oven, and closed the door.

She stood on her tip toes to check the top of the stove and looked directly into the mirror with a big smile. She stooped down, opened the oven door, removed the cupcakes, and walked back to the table. At the table, she stood and squeezed the play dough in a cup. She looked over at T. and said, "He can have one."

Doris Sponseller
Oakland University

A Schema for Play and for Learning

There are many ways of looking at play and learning. When we try to define either of these concepts, we are reminded of the old story of the blind men who wanted to know what an elephant was. When they approached the elephant, each one of them took hold of a different part. The one who touched the tail said, "Why, an elephant is long and thin and wiggly, just like a snake." The one who touched the leg objected, saying "No, no, an elephant is sturdy and round, similar to a tree," while the one who touched the ear stated that, in fact, "The elephant is exactly like a big, floppy leaf." And, of course, those who touched the side, the tusk, and the trunk had equally definite descriptions and were equally sure that their conception of an elephant was the correct one.

Those who have studied play and learning have often run into a similar dilemma. There are many descriptions, each of which probably is some part of the truth, but which are also dependent upon which portion the theorist has chosen for focus. For example, Piaget (1962) has looked at play primarily as it relates to the logical structures of knowledge, while Erikson (1963) has seen play as having prime importance in the mastery of emotional needs. In the

115

same way, learning to Skinner (1968) is a completely observable phenomenon, while to Ausubel (1968) learning is only meaningful when discussed in terms of the inner structures of the mind. Each of the persons who have studied play and/or learning have probably described one part of the "elephant," but many more parts are still in need of observational and experimental research before the whole animal can be outlined. It can be useful, however, to develop an overall schema into which play and learning can be categorized.

We begin from the broadest premise: Play is observable behavior, but it is also nonobservable behavior. We know the first is so because countless observers have described behaviors which they label play. But, we also know from our own experience that play is not always observable. All of us have played mentally, sometimes when we deliberately allowed our ideas to go into disequillibrium (creativity), to play with ideas, but also at times when we should have been listening or reading for meaning, we have found that our minds might begin playing (daydreaming) rather than attending to our initial goal.

Also, although play is usually of a physically active quality, some play behaviors fall into the physically passive realm. Onlooking behavior in which the watcher may be mentally active but appears to be uninvolved physically is of this type. Much of what adults call entertainment can be thought of as physically passive play behavior.

Play is sometimes called free and sometimes called guided or directed. Free play is not entirely free, however, since there are still rules which govern the play interactions. Usually these rules are imposed by the materials (for example, block towers fall if not balanced properly) or by the player's physical or mental qualities (such as the eye/hand coordination needed for completing a puzzle). Guided or directed play usually has a social element which regulates the rules governing the play. This may be from rules related to other players or from social rules imposed by the culture. Quite often elements of both natural and social rules are evident in the same play behavior. These elements of play occur in the activities of adults as well as those of children. However, less of adult play is observable, and much of that which is observable is called by some other name.

Play throughout life

Herron and Sutton-Smith (1971) define play as "an exercise of voluntary control systems with disequillibrial outcomes" (p. 344). They contend that play is not only a phenomenon of childhood but that it is present throughout life, merely taking different forms. We might say that the tendency to playfulness is inherent in human beings, but that its manifestations vary with cultural expectations of appropriate behaviors and with developmental changes (such as the gradual predominance of logical thought structure at successive age levels). In other words, play may be genotypically the same throughout life but phenotypically different. At certain ages it is appropriate to call certain behaviors play, but at other times they must be called by other names. For example, adults usually are not considered as participants in sociodramatic play. However, they participate in role simulations, drama, talk sessions, political conventions, and even work in which large elements of sociodramatic play are evident. As Sutton-Smith says, "Is the 'reality' of chess or football more real than the reality of 'bogeyman?' Or is it simply that as adults we are more familiar with our own ludic forms?" (p. 301).

As with other inherent characteristics, it is possible for persons to be less well developed in their growth in relation to play behaviors. However, this does not mean that play is not a necessary part of human existence. There are many physically and intellectually thwarted individuals, but we do not deny the need for facilitating physical and intellectual development. Therefore, it is important for us to recognize the play potential that each of us has, because if play is seen as something which is only apparent in childhood, it will be considered by adults to be immature, inconsequential, and therefore something to be outgrown. As teachers we cannot value play in children if we do not also value play in adults. If we do not value play as a human behavior which is essential at all ages and at all levels of development, we will not see its tremendous value as a medium for learning or as a medium for anything.

Learning throughout life

In utilizing play as a medium for learning in the educational setting, it is also necessary to look at various types of learning which have been identified by learning theorists.

Theorists who are concerned with higher cognitive processes, such as Ausubel, Piaget, Gagné, and Bruner, have classified types of learning in various ways. All of them seem to be in agreement, however, that learning which occurs through classical or operant conditioning is not a sufficient explanation for the type of learning involving the higher cognitive processes.

They stress various types of learning as being most essential for these higher processes to develop

118

optimally. For example, Bruner (1973) posits the view that the kind of learning in which the person takes an active discovery role and develops strategies for problem solving is the type of learning which is essential for the growth of complex cognitive structures.

Ausubel (1968) recognizes discovery learning with concrete objects to be important to young children who have not yet developed these cognitive structures. However, he sees reception learning or meaningful verbal learning to be more appropriate and efficient for older children and adults. He distinguishes emphatically between this meaningful verbal learning and the rote verbal learning which has been studied extensively by behavioral psychologists. To Ausubel, verbal learning is only meaningful when the cognitive structures are sufficiently developed so that the information can be mentally organized or subsumed by the individual. These structures are usually developed between the ages of six and eight.

Piaget's views of the most effective methods of learning have been discussed previously by other contributors to this book. He, too, stresses the importance of what might be called a discovery learning approach in the young child.

Wason and Johnson (1968), who have been specifically interested in problem solving, report on studies which have examined the characteristics of adults who are good problem solvers. In general these studies conclude that adults are hampered in solving problems if they have previously known only one use for an object, or if they have learned by rote a particular method for solving a type of problem. Thus, even in adults, the ability to play with the object or concept is a prerequisite for discovery learning and utilization or invention of strategies for problem solving.

The play and learning continuum

Since there are many behaviors which can be called play and many behaviors which can be called learning, it seems appropriate to attempt to differentiate them in some manner and determine their interrelationship before we can utilize play as a learning medium in the classroom. Two dimensions by which they can be differentiated that are important for teachers to consider are the degree to which active adult guidance is provided, and whether the area of emphasis is on process or product. This enables us to develop a continuum of play and learning behaviors (Figure 1) ranging from those which have little adult intervention and very broadly defined and often unstated adult goals, to those which are highly structured by adults or society and which have definite goals either stated or unstated.

Figure 1

**The Continuum of Play and Learning Activities
and Their Interrelationship**

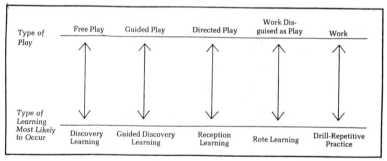

Many educators do not recognize any activity as play except the free play type. However, most teachers utilize different types of play during the course of a school day. Usually some activities are of guided or gamelike types directed with the teacher as leader. Teachers who are working in an academically oriented setting primarily direct their energies to

120

presenting work as play; for example, some language-based programs utilize rote responses and repetition, other programs reject play as having any part in the curriculum. The activities in the Montessori program are labeled as work rather than play. In the framework developed here, however, the Montessori program would be labeled guided play with the guidance and structure coming primarily from the structure of the environment and materials. Thus, the play continuum ranges from behaviors identified as free play to behaviors identified as work.

The teacher can use all of these types of play to further goals. Where the emphasis is placed depends on the developmental level of the child, the theoretical orientation of the teacher, and the objectives of the school and culture. If the culture or school select the goals, the teacher should be able to choose the modes most in harmony with individual children's abilities and needs.

In analyzing a learning activity, or in observing a play behavior, the schema can be utilized to determine the probable interrelationship between the type of learning and the type of play. For example, if the goal of the teacher is to develop problem-solving skills through a discovery learning approach, free or guided play would be an appropriate medium for this learning.

A loosely organized group game, for which initial direction is given by the teacher but in which children's interaction is primarily self-directed, would be classified as guided play, since the goal is to enable children to discover relationships and develop cognitive skills.

Play in which the teacher is leader throughout the activity is considered directed play; it may provide aspects of discovery learning, but usually includes reception learning in which the verbalizations are meaningful because of the child's past experiences.

Teachers have often used methods which incorporate elements of play if memorization of a rote verbal nature is desired, such as the learning of the letters of the alphabet in sequence. Whether teachers should or should not disguise work as play is, of course, a debatable point. This technique has long been used in classrooms to make a necessary task more enjoyable. We must recognize what these activities really are, however, and not expect them to meet the total play needs of the child.

This book has been primarily concerned with free or guided types of play since the higher cognitive processes are major concerns of the authors. These types of play appear to provide the best media for the kinds of learning which are considered important for the young child's optimal cognitive, social, and emotional development.

On the other hand, there is certainly room in the early childhood curriculum for fingerplays, songs, and other teacher-directed play activities. It may even be appropriate to include work disguised as play. It is essential, however, that a major portion of the young child's school day be set aside specifically for free or guided play and that the teacher realize and facilitate discovery learning and development of problem-solving strategies through the medium of play.

This development can be facilitated by designing an environment which encourages free and guided play, and by utilizing other types of play when the learning desired makes them appropriate. Teachers must also value their own playfulness, and recognize and nurture play as an important medium for learning for both children and adults.

References

Ausubel, D. P. *Educational Psychology: A Cognitive View.* New York: Holt, Rinehart & Winston, 1968.

Bruner, J. S. *Beyond the Information Given.* New York: W. W. Norton, 1973.

Erikson, E. H. *Childhood & Society.* New York: W. W. Norton, 1963.

Herron, R. E. and Sutton-Smith, B., *Child's Play.* New York: John Wiley & Sons, 1971.

Piaget, J. *Play, Dreams, and Imitation in Childhood.* New York: W. W. Norton and Co., 1962.

Skinner, B. F. *The Technology of Teaching.* New York: Appleton-Century-Crofts, 1968.

Wason, P. C. and Johnson-Laird, P. N. *Thinking & Reasoning.* Baltimore, Md.: Penquin, 1968.

Selected NAEYC Publications

Code	Title	Price
214	Activities for School-Age Child Care	$3.50
303	A Beginner's Bibliography	$ .50
132	The Block Book	$3.50
213	Caring: Supporting Children's Growth	$2.00
402S	Cómo Reconocer un Buen Programa de Educación Pre-Escolar	$ .25
313	Cultural Awareness: A Resource Bibliography	$4.75
104	Current Issues in Child Development	$3.50
119	Curriculum Is What Happens	$2.00
125	Demythologizing the Inner-City Child	$4.00
121	Developmental Screening in Early Childhood: A Guide	$2.50
112	Ethical Behavior in Early Childhood Education	$1.75
215	A Festival of Films	$1.75
302	A Guide to Discipline, revised edition	$1.50
210	The Idea Box	$5.75
304	Ideas That Work with Young Children	$3.00
130	Imagination: Key to Human Potential	$3.50
131	Language in Early Childhood Education	$3.00
101	Let's Play Outdoors	$1.00
312	Mother/Child, Father/Child Relationships	$4.75
308	Mud, Sand, and Water	$2.00
135	Parent Involvement in Early Childhood Education	$3.00
102	Piaget, Children, and Number	$2.00
115	Planning Environments for Young Children: Physical Space	$1.75
129	Play: The Child Strives Toward Self-Realization	$2.50
126	Promoting Cognitive Growth	$2.75
307	Providing the Best for Young Children	$3.25
309	Science with Young Children	$3.25
128	The Significance of the Young Child's Motor Development	$2.25
402E	Some Ways of Distinguishing a Good Early Childhood Program	$ .25
310	Talks with Teachers: Reflections on Early Childhood Education	$3.00

Order from NAEYC
1834 Connecticut Avenue, N.W.
Washington, DC 20009

For information about these and other NAEYC publications, write for a free publications brochure.

Please enclose full payment for orders under $10.00. Add 10% handling charge to all orders.